PEARSON ALWAYS LEARNING

Mark Solomonovich

The Space of Geometric Vectors and Analytic Geometry of Lines and Planes

Grant MacEwan University

Cover Art: *Dome*, by Angela Sciaraffa, *Boatbu1*, by Barry Cronin

Pearson Learning Solutions, 501 Boylston Street, Suite 900, Boston, MA 02116
A Pearson Education Company
www.pearsoned.com

Printed in Canada

3 4 5 6 7 8 9 10 V0CR 16 15 14 13 12

000200010270792650

MHB

PEARSON

ISBN 10: 1-256-35617-4
ISBN 13: 978-1-256-35617-2

TABLE OF CONTENTS

I. THE SPACE OF GEOMETRIC VECTORS AND ANALYTIC GEOMETRY OF LINES AND PLANES.

1. LINEAR OPERATIONS WITH GEOMETRIC VECTORS.

1.1 GEOMETRIC VECTORS: BASIC NOTIONS.

In Linear Algebra we deal with two kinds of objects: *scalars*, which are just numbers (in this course we shall mean *real numbers*), and *vectors* that are such objects for which the so-called *linear operations* can be defined. The latter ones are called the *scalar multiplication* (multiplication of a vector by a number) and the *addition of vectors*, and they are defined as operations that possess certain properties, which are not dissimilar to the well-known properties of ordinary multiplication and addition as defined for numbers.

There is a great variety of kinds of vectors: geometric vectors, physical vectors, ordered arrays of numbers, polynomials, to name just a few, and the only thing they all have in common are the linear operations and their properties. They are the same for any set of vectors, no matter what is the nature of the vectors considered in a specific case. We shall list these properties and discuss them in detail later on in the course.

In general, vectors are more complicated objects than scalars: a vector, in general, cannot be defined with just a single number. For instance, in physics, length, mass, density, energy are scalars, – each of them can be identified as a number in given units, whereas such characteristics as displacement, velocity, force, torque, are vectors, – each of them is defined by its magnitude (a number) and its direction or by an ordered set of several numbers.

We shall start our discussion with the simplest example of vectors, – the so-called *geometric vectors*. This example will allow us to visualize the most important notions of linear algebra and to develop certain techniques that will turn out to be useful in the consideration of general vector spaces and in applications of linear algebra.

Definition. A geometric vector is a *directed segment*: one endpoint of such a segment is considered to be the *origin* (*initial point*, *tail*) whereas the other one is the *end* (*terminal point*, *tip*) of the vector. A directed segment whose terminal point coincides with its origin is also a vector; it is called a *zero vector*.

We shall denote a vector with a two-letter symbol with an arrow above the letters, where the first letter signifies the origin. An alternate notation is a single lowercase letter with an arrow or just a single lowercase letter printed in boldface. For example, the vectors in Figure1 are denoted as $\overrightarrow{AC} = \boldsymbol{a}$, $\overrightarrow{BD} = \boldsymbol{b}$, and $\overrightarrow{MN} = \boldsymbol{u}$ respectively.

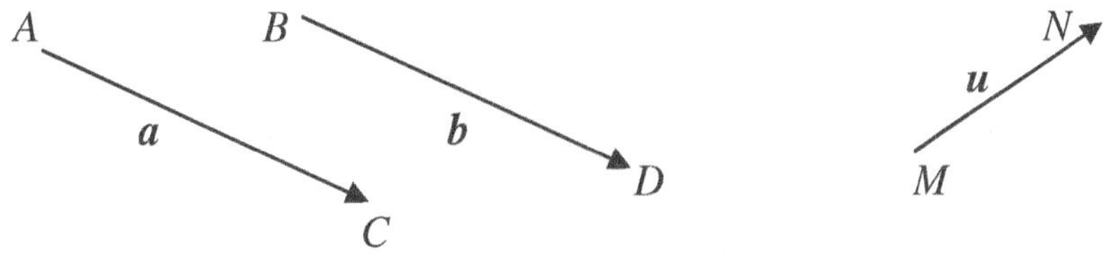

Figure 1

A zero vector is denoted by the zero symbol with an arrow or printed in boldface. If, for example, A is a point in space, then $\overrightarrow{AA}$ is a zero vector: $\overrightarrow{AA} = \boldsymbol{0}$ (In handwriting we usually use arrows: $\overrightarrow{AA} = \vec{0}$). Note that the $\boldsymbol{0}$ in the right-hand side of the last two equalities is not the number zero but a vector!

Each vector is defined by two characteristics: its *length*, which is also called the *norm* or *magnitude*, and its *direction*. Let us discuss each of these.

We suggest that the unit of length is chosen and all the segments are measured on the same scale. Then every vector can be assigned a nonnegative real number that expresses the length of the segment corresponding to this vector. This number is usually called the *norm of the vector*, and denoted by the $\| \ \|$ symbol. If, for example, the length of segment AB is equal to 5 units of length, we will say that the norm of $\overrightarrow{AB}$ equals 5 and express it as $\left\|\overrightarrow{AB}\right\| = 5$.

The norm of a *zero vector* is zero by definition: $\|\boldsymbol{0}\| = 0$. The direction of a zero vector is not defined, therefore one can assign to a zero vector any direction.

In order to identify nonzero vectors according to their *directions*, we shall introduce a few notions. Two vectors are said to be *collinear* if they lie on the same line or on parallel lines. For instance, in Figure 2, $\boldsymbol{a}$ is collinear with $\boldsymbol{b}$, $\boldsymbol{b}$ is collinear with $\boldsymbol{c}$, $\boldsymbol{a}$ is collinear with $\boldsymbol{c}$, and any of these three is collinear with $\boldsymbol{d}$, whereas $\boldsymbol{u}$ is not collinear with any of these four vectors.

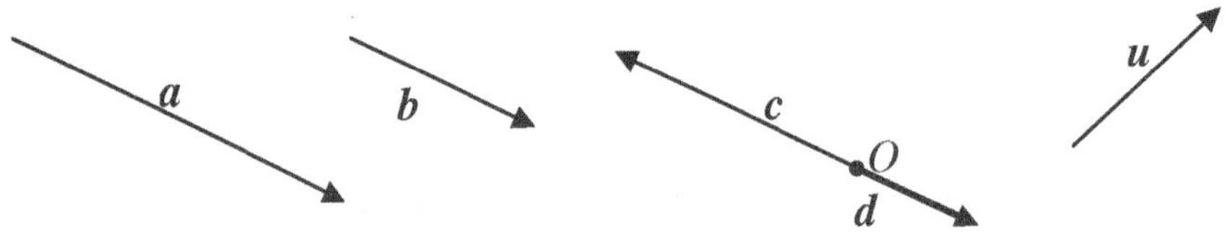

Figure 2

Collinear vectors can be *co-directed* (or *parallel*) like, for example, vectors $\boldsymbol{a}$ and $\boldsymbol{b}$ in Figure 2, or *oppositely directed* (*antiparallel*) like vectors $\boldsymbol{b}$ and $\boldsymbol{c}$ (or $\boldsymbol{d}$ and $\boldsymbol{c}$) in the same figure. We shall denote such relations by the $\uparrow\uparrow$ and $\downarrow\uparrow$ symbols. For example, in Figure 2, $\boldsymbol{a} \uparrow\uparrow \boldsymbol{b}$; $\boldsymbol{b} \downarrow\uparrow \boldsymbol{c}$. In order to define the relations of vectors being *co-directed* (or *parallel*) and *oppositely directed* (*antiparallel*), we have to consider two possible cases: (i) collinear vectors lie on the same line, and (ii) collinear vectors lie on parallel lines.

In case (i), we slide one of the vectors along the line in which they lie until its origin coincides with the origin of another vector (like, for example, the origins of vectors $\boldsymbol{d}$ and $\boldsymbol{c}$ in the above figure). Then we shall say that the vectors are *co-directed* if their endpoints lie on the same side from the common origin; otherwise we shall call them *oppositely directed.*

In case (ii), we shall draw a line through their origins. This line divides the plane in which the vectors lie into two half-planes. Then we shall call two collinear vectors *co-directed* if their terminal points lie in the same half-planes, and *oppositely directed* otherwise (i.e. the terminal points of two *antiparallel* vectors lie on the opposite sides of the straight line passing through their origins).

These definitions are illustrated in Figure 3.

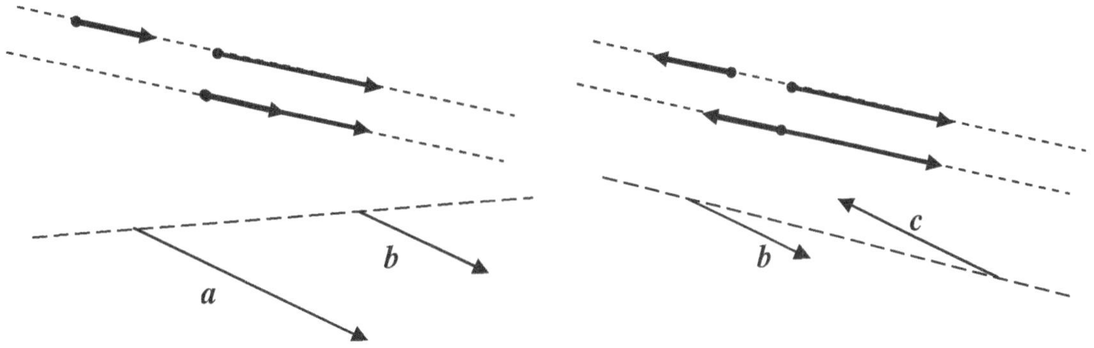

Parallel vectors (collinear and co-directed)

Antiparallel vectors (collinear and oppositely directed)

Figure 3

Definition. Two vectors are said to be *equal* if they are parallel (collinear and co-directed) and their lengths are equal.

It follows from this definition that a vector can be *translated parallel to itself*. It means the following. Having given a point C in space and some vector $\overrightarrow{AB}$, we can construct such a vector $\overrightarrow{CD}$ originating at C that $\overrightarrow{CD} \uparrow\uparrow \overrightarrow{AB}$ and $\left\|\overrightarrow{CD}\right\| = \left\|\overrightarrow{AB}\right\|$. Then, by definition, $\overrightarrow{CD} = \overrightarrow{AB}$, and thus it can be viewed as $\overrightarrow{AB}$ that has been *translated parallel to itself* so as to have C as the origin.

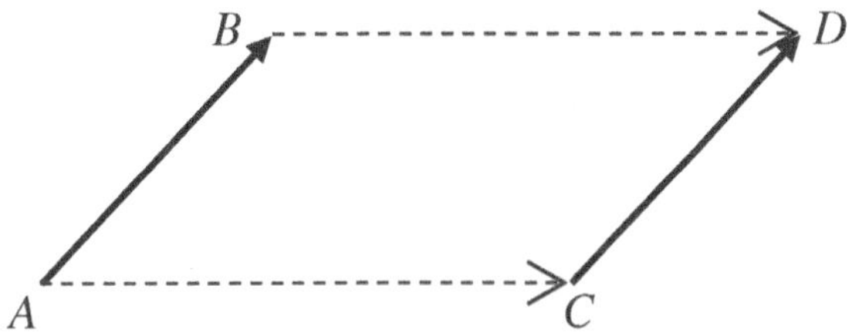

Figure 4

Figure 4 illustrates the operation of the translation of a vector. The figure $ABCD$ obtained by joining the origin and the end of the original vector ($\overrightarrow{AB}$) with the origin and the end respectively of its *image* ($\overrightarrow{CD}$), is a parallelogram (since $AB \,||\, CD$ and their length are equal). It is easy to show that $ABCD$ is not a parallelogram if $\overrightarrow{CD} \neq \overrightarrow{AB}$. Thus, $ABCD$ is a parallelogram *if and only if* $\overrightarrow{CD} = \overrightarrow{AB}$, i.e. it is a parallelogram if they are equal, and it is not a parallelogram if they are not.

Let us also notice that a translation of a vector itself is determined by a vector joining the origin of the vector with the origin of its *image* obtained as a result of the translation. For instance, in the above example, the translation is defined by vector $\overrightarrow{AC}$ or equal to it vector $\overrightarrow{BD}$.

1.2 LINEAR OPERATIONS WITH GEOMETRIC VECTORS.

Now we shall define the operations of addition of vectors and multiplication of a vector by a real number and study properties of these operations.

Definition. Let $\boldsymbol{a}$ and $\boldsymbol{b}$ be two vectors. Translate vector $\boldsymbol{b}$ so that it originates at the terminal point of $\boldsymbol{a}$. Then the vector that emanates from the origin of $\boldsymbol{a}$ and ends at the terminal point of $\boldsymbol{b}$, is called the *sum of* $\boldsymbol{a}$ *and* $\boldsymbol{b}$ and denoted $\boldsymbol{a}+\boldsymbol{b}$.

For example, in Figure 1a, $\boldsymbol{a}+\boldsymbol{b}=\overrightarrow{AB}+\overrightarrow{BC}=\overrightarrow{AC}$. The above definition is usually called the *triangle rule.*

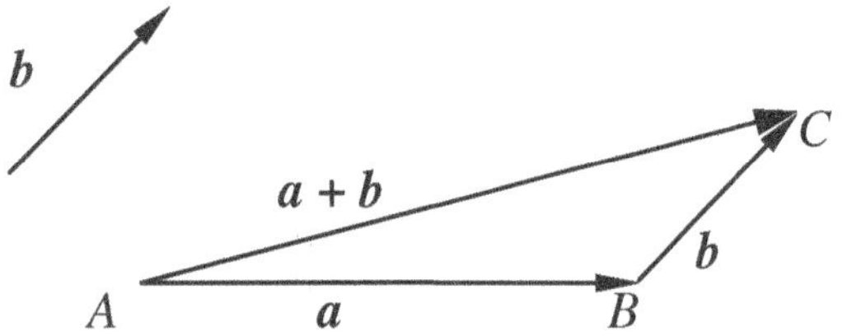

Figure 1a

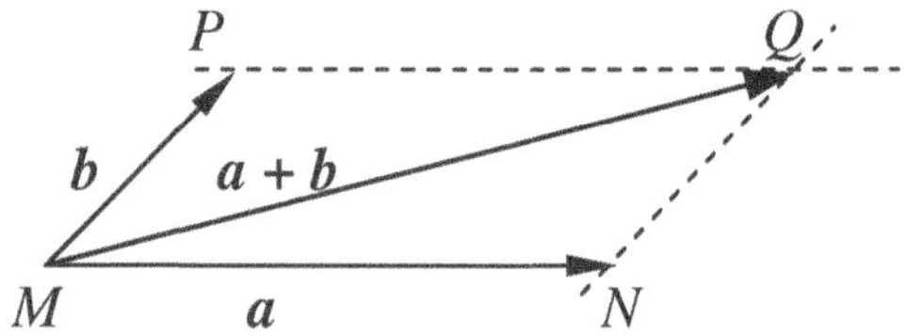

Figure 1b

An equivalent way of constructing $\boldsymbol{a}+\boldsymbol{b}$ is shown in Figure 1b. Translate vectors $\boldsymbol{a}$ and $\boldsymbol{b}$ in such positions that they origins coincide. Now the two vectors emanate from the same point (point M in Figure 1b). Then, through the terminal points of $\boldsymbol{a}$ and $\boldsymbol{b}$ (points N and P in our figure), draw lines parallel to $\boldsymbol{b}$ and $\boldsymbol{a}$ respectively. They will intersect at some point Q. It is easy to show that vector $\overrightarrow{MQ}$ is equal to the vector $\overrightarrow{AC}$ in Figure 1, and therefore $\overrightarrow{MQ}=\boldsymbol{a}+\boldsymbol{b}$. This method of constructing the sum of two vectors is called the *parallelogram rule.*

Based on the definition, we can show (*show* is the synonym of *prove*) that the operation of vector addition possesses the following properties.

(1) For any vectors $\boldsymbol{a}$ and $\boldsymbol{b}$, $\boldsymbol{a}+\boldsymbol{b}=\boldsymbol{b}+\boldsymbol{a}$ *(commutative law of addition).*
(2) For any vectors $\boldsymbol{a}$, $\boldsymbol{b}$, and $\boldsymbol{c}$, $\boldsymbol{a}+(\boldsymbol{b}+\boldsymbol{c})=(\boldsymbol{a}+\boldsymbol{b})+\boldsymbol{c}$ *(associative law of addition).*
(3) For any vector $\boldsymbol{a}$, $\boldsymbol{a}+\boldsymbol{0}=\boldsymbol{a}$ *(the existence of zero).*
(4) For any vector $\boldsymbol{a}$, there exists such a vector $-\boldsymbol{a}$, that $\boldsymbol{a}+(-\boldsymbol{a})=\boldsymbol{0}$ *(the existence of the opposite, or additive inverse).*

Let us prove these properties.

(1) It follows immediately from the definition. In Figure 1b, $\overrightarrow{MQ}=\overrightarrow{MP}+\overrightarrow{PQ}=\boldsymbol{b}+\boldsymbol{a}$. On the other hand, $\overrightarrow{MQ}=\overrightarrow{MN}+\overrightarrow{NQ}=\boldsymbol{a}+\boldsymbol{b}$. Thus, $\overrightarrow{MQ}=\boldsymbol{b}+\boldsymbol{a}=\boldsymbol{a}+\boldsymbol{b}$.
(2) Translate if necessary vectors $\boldsymbol{b}$ and $\boldsymbol{c}$ so that $\boldsymbol{b}$ originates at the terminal point of $\boldsymbol{a}$, and the origin of $\boldsymbol{c}$ is located at the terminal point of $\boldsymbol{b}$. Then,

each of the sums, $\boldsymbol{a}+(\boldsymbol{b}+\boldsymbol{c})$ and $(\boldsymbol{a}+\boldsymbol{b})+\boldsymbol{c}$, is presented by the same vector: the one emanating from the origin of $\boldsymbol{a}$ and ending at the terminal point of $\boldsymbol{c}$. (One can also see the illustration in the figure below, though it is not necessary).

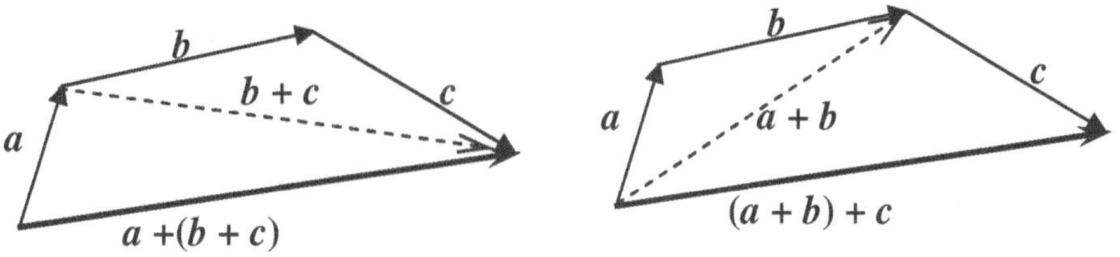

Figure 2

(3) If $\boldsymbol{a}=\overrightarrow{AB}$, let $\boldsymbol{0}=\overrightarrow{BB}$, then $\boldsymbol{a}+\boldsymbol{0}=\overrightarrow{AB}+\overrightarrow{BB}=\overrightarrow{AB}=\boldsymbol{a}$.
(4) If $\boldsymbol{a}=\overrightarrow{AB}$, let $-\boldsymbol{a}=\overrightarrow{BA}$, then $\boldsymbol{a}+(-\boldsymbol{a})=\overrightarrow{AB}+\overrightarrow{BA}=\overrightarrow{AA}=\boldsymbol{0}$.

As in the ordinary arithmetic of numbers, the *subtraction* is not an independent operation: it can be defined through addition. Vector $\boldsymbol{d}$ will be called the *difference* between $\boldsymbol{a}$ and $\boldsymbol{b}$, and we shall write $\boldsymbol{d}=\boldsymbol{a}-\boldsymbol{b}$ if $\boldsymbol{b}+\boldsymbol{d}=\boldsymbol{a}$ (see the diagram in Figure 3).

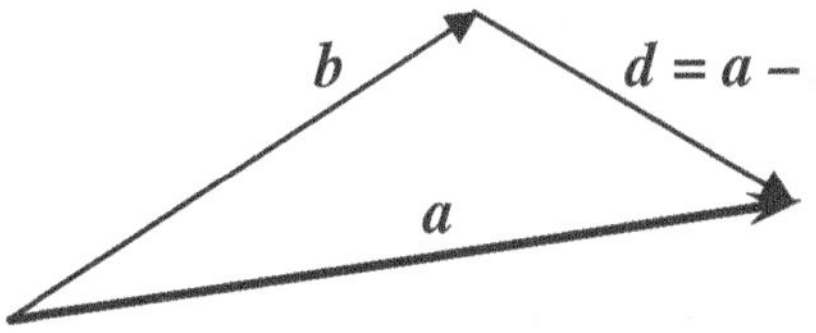

Figure 3

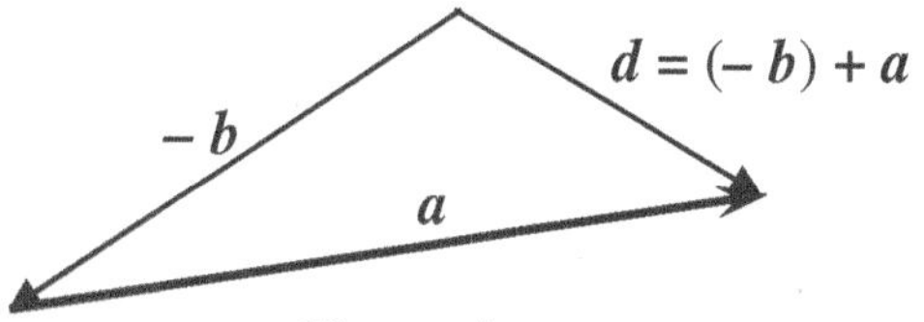

Figure 4

Also, as one can see from Figure 4, the subtraction of a vector can be viewed as the addition of the opposite of this vector: $\boldsymbol{d}=\boldsymbol{a}-\boldsymbol{b}=(-\boldsymbol{b})+\boldsymbol{a}=\boldsymbol{a}+(-\boldsymbol{b})$ (the subtraction of $\boldsymbol{b}$ is equivalent to the addition of $-\boldsymbol{b}$). This view of subtraction turns out to be convenient in some practical problems.

Example 1. For the vectors shown in Figure 5, express vector $\boldsymbol{v}$ through the vectors $\boldsymbol{a}$, $\boldsymbol{b}$, $\boldsymbol{c}$, $\boldsymbol{d}$, and $\boldsymbol{e}$.

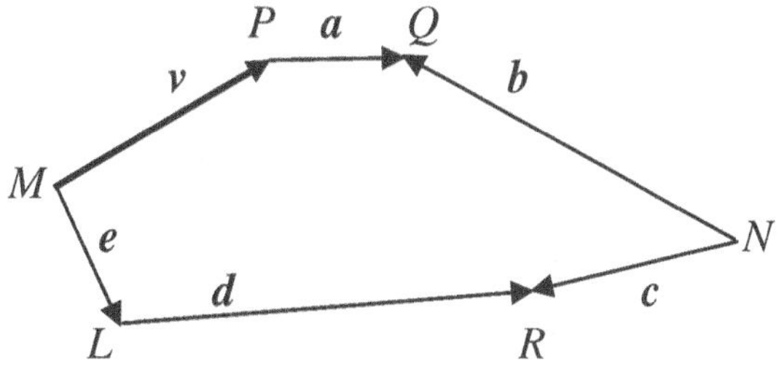

Figure 5

Solution 1. Let us join M with N by a vector $\overrightarrow{MN}$ (Figure 6). Then we can express this vector in the following ways:

$\overrightarrow{MN} = \overrightarrow{MP} + \overrightarrow{PQ} + \overrightarrow{QN} = \boldsymbol{v} + \boldsymbol{a} + (-\boldsymbol{b})$, and

$\overrightarrow{MN} = \overrightarrow{ML} + \overrightarrow{LR} + \overrightarrow{RN} = \boldsymbol{e} + \boldsymbol{d} + (-\boldsymbol{c})$.

Therefore, $\overrightarrow{MN} = \boldsymbol{v} + \boldsymbol{a} + (-\boldsymbol{b}) = \boldsymbol{e} + \boldsymbol{d} + (-\boldsymbol{c})$. By adding $(-\boldsymbol{a}) + \boldsymbol{b}$ to the both sides of the last equality, we obtain: $\boldsymbol{v} = (-\boldsymbol{a}) + \boldsymbol{b} + \boldsymbol{e} + \boldsymbol{d} + (-\boldsymbol{c})$, or simply

$\boldsymbol{v} = \boldsymbol{e} + \boldsymbol{d} + \boldsymbol{b} - \boldsymbol{a} - \boldsymbol{c}$.

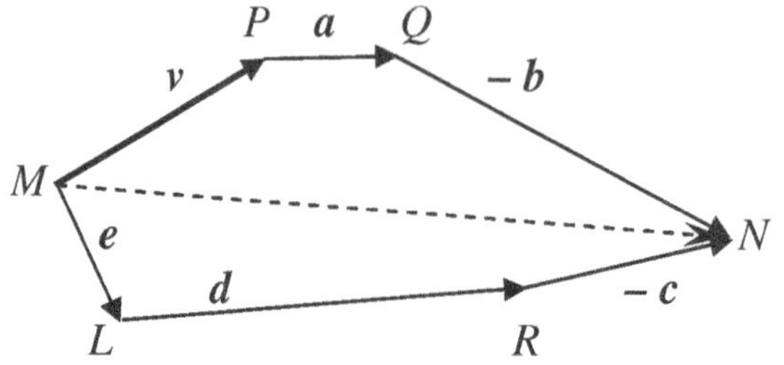

Figure 6

Solution 2. $\overrightarrow{MM} = \boldsymbol{v} + \boldsymbol{a} + (-\boldsymbol{b}) + \boldsymbol{c} + (-\boldsymbol{d}) + (-\boldsymbol{e}) = \boldsymbol{0}$, whence

$\boldsymbol{v} = -\boldsymbol{a} + \boldsymbol{b} - \boldsymbol{c} + \boldsymbol{d} + \boldsymbol{e}$, or $\boldsymbol{v} = \boldsymbol{e} + \boldsymbol{d} + \boldsymbol{b} - \boldsymbol{a} - \boldsymbol{c}$.

(Hereafter we shall write similar expressions, the so-called *algebraic sums of vectors*, without brackets, like in the latter two equalities. It is clear that, e.g., $-\boldsymbol{a} + \boldsymbol{b}$ means the addition of the opposite of **a** to **b**, or the subtraction of **a** out of **b**. As for the order of addition, the brackets are not necessary due to the associative law.)

Definition. Let α be a number (real number) and **a** be a vector. Then $\alpha\boldsymbol{a}$, called the *scalar multiple* of **a** with the coefficient α, is such a vector that

$\|\alpha\boldsymbol{a}\| = |\alpha| \cdot \|\boldsymbol{a}\|$, and

$\alpha\boldsymbol{a} \uparrow\uparrow \boldsymbol{a}$ if $\alpha > 0$, and $\alpha\boldsymbol{a} \downarrow\uparrow \boldsymbol{a}$ if $\alpha < 0$.

It should be noticed that the second part of the definition does not include the case of $\alpha = 0$ since in this case, according to the first part, $\|\alpha\boldsymbol{a}\| = 0$, and $\alpha\boldsymbol{a}$ is a zero vector, whose direction cannot be determined.

A few examples illustrating the above definition of *scalar multiplication* are shown in Figure 7.

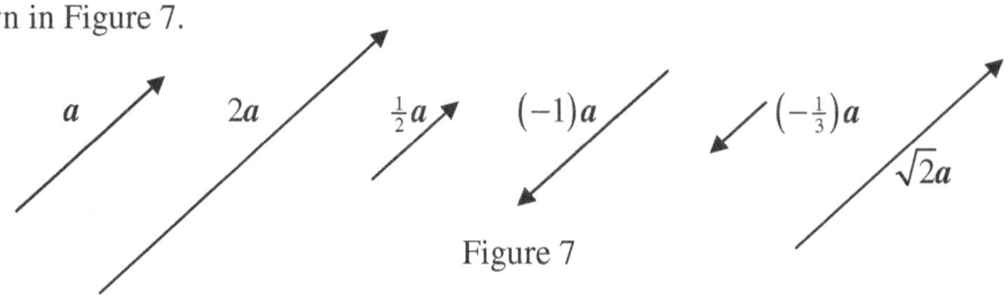

Figure 7

It follows from the above definition that if two vectors are *proportional* (i.e. one of them is a *scalar multiple* of the other), then they are collinear. What if we have two collinear vectors: are they necessarily proportional?

It turns out that this statement (called the *converse* of the original statement) is also true: if two vectors are collinear, then they are proportional, i.e. one of them can be obtained from the other by means of multiplication by a scalar. Let us formulate this result, together with the original statement, as a theorem and prove it.

Theorem 1.2.1 Two vectors are proportional, i.e. one of them is a scalar multiple of the other, if and only if they are collinear.

Proof. This theorem consists of two statements that can be briefly presented as follows:

(1) vectors are collinear $\Rightarrow$ they are proportional (collinearity implies proportionality);

(2) vectors are proportional $\Rightarrow$ they are collinear (proportionality implies collinearity).

(One is the original, or *direct* statement, and (2) – its *converse*).

Let us start with the proof of the first statement.

Suppose $\boldsymbol{u}$ and $\boldsymbol{a}$ are two proportional vectors, i.e. $\boldsymbol{u} = \alpha \boldsymbol{a}$, where α is some scalar (number). Then by the definition of scalar multiplication, they are collinear. Thus we have shown that proportionality implies collinearity

Now let us suppose that $\boldsymbol{a}$ is some vector and $\boldsymbol{u}$ is collinear with $\boldsymbol{a}$. The following two cases are possible: (i) $\boldsymbol{a} = \boldsymbol{0}$ and (ii) $\boldsymbol{a} \neq \boldsymbol{0}$.

In case (i) $\boldsymbol{a} = \boldsymbol{0}$ (which makes sense since a zero vector has no definite direction and is therefore collinear with any vector), we can write $\boldsymbol{a} = 0 \cdot \boldsymbol{u}$, which means that $\boldsymbol{a}$ is proportional to $\boldsymbol{u}$; this proves the statement. It is interesting to notice that in this case $\boldsymbol{a}$ is a scalar multiple of $\boldsymbol{u}$, but $\boldsymbol{u}$ is not a scalar multiple of $\boldsymbol{a}$!

In the second case, $\boldsymbol{a} \neq \boldsymbol{0}$, we choose

$\alpha = \frac{\|\boldsymbol{u}\|}{\|\boldsymbol{a}\|}$ if $\boldsymbol{u} \uparrow\uparrow \boldsymbol{a}$, and $\alpha = -\frac{\|\boldsymbol{u}\|}{\|\boldsymbol{a}\|}$ if $\boldsymbol{u} \downarrow\uparrow \boldsymbol{a}$. Then $\boldsymbol{u} = \alpha \boldsymbol{a}$. Really, in any of these cases $\alpha \boldsymbol{a} \uparrow\uparrow \boldsymbol{u}$, and $\|\alpha \boldsymbol{a}\| = |\alpha| \|\boldsymbol{a}\| = \frac{\|\boldsymbol{u}\|}{\|\boldsymbol{a}\|} \cdot \|\boldsymbol{a}\| = \|\boldsymbol{u}\|$. □

Now we can complete the list of the basic properties of linear operations on vectors. The operation of multiplication by numbers possesses two such properties of its own (the scaling property and the associative law) and another two in combination with the addition of vectors (the distributive laws):

(5) For any vector $\boldsymbol{a}$, $1 \cdot \boldsymbol{a} = \boldsymbol{a}$ *(scaling property)*

(6) For any vector $\boldsymbol{a}$ and any numbers α, β, $(\alpha\beta)\boldsymbol{a} = \alpha(\beta \boldsymbol{a})$ *(associative law)*

(7) For any vector $\boldsymbol{a}$ and any numbers α, β, $(\alpha + \beta)\boldsymbol{a} = \alpha \boldsymbol{a} + \beta \boldsymbol{a}$ *(distributive law)*

(8) For any vectors $\boldsymbol{a}$ and $\boldsymbol{b}$ and any number α, $\alpha(\boldsymbol{a} + \boldsymbol{b}) = \alpha \boldsymbol{a} + \alpha \boldsymbol{b}$ *(distributive law).*

We shall prove some of these properties, leaving the rest as exercises for students.

In order to prove property (6) we have to show that the vectors $(\alpha\beta)\boldsymbol{a}$ and $\alpha(\beta\boldsymbol{a})$ have the same length and are parallel (collinear and co-directed). By definition, $\|(\alpha\beta)\boldsymbol{a}\| = |\alpha\beta| \cdot \|\boldsymbol{a}\|$, and $\|\alpha(\beta\boldsymbol{a})\| = |\alpha| \cdot \|\beta\boldsymbol{a}\| = |\alpha| \cdot |\beta| \cdot \|\boldsymbol{a}\|$. By properties of the absolute value, $|\alpha| \cdot |\beta| = |\alpha\beta|$, therefore $|\alpha| \cdot |\beta| \cdot \|\boldsymbol{a}\| = |\alpha\beta| \cdot \boldsymbol{a}$, and as a result, $\|\alpha(\beta\boldsymbol{a})\| = \|(\alpha\beta)\boldsymbol{a}\|$.

Now let us show that vectors $(\alpha\beta)\boldsymbol{a}$ and $\alpha(\beta\boldsymbol{a})$are parallel. We shall have to consider the following four possible cases:

(i) $\alpha > 0, \beta > 0$; (ii) $\alpha > 0, \beta < 0$; (iii) $\alpha < 0, \beta > 0$; (iv)$\alpha < 0, \beta < 0$.

(i) If $\alpha > 0, \beta > 0$, then $\alpha\beta > 0$, hence, $(\alpha\beta)\boldsymbol{a} \uparrow\uparrow \boldsymbol{a}$. Also, since $\beta > 0$, $\beta\boldsymbol{a} \uparrow\uparrow \boldsymbol{a}$, and then $\alpha(\beta\boldsymbol{a}) \uparrow\uparrow \beta\boldsymbol{a} \uparrow\uparrow \boldsymbol{a}$. Therefore, each of the two vectors is parallel to ***a***, and hence they are parallel: $(\alpha\beta)\boldsymbol{a} \uparrow\uparrow \alpha(\beta\boldsymbol{a})$.

(ii) In case $\alpha > 0, \beta < 0$, their product is negative: $\alpha\beta < 0$, hence, $(\alpha\beta)\boldsymbol{a} \downarrow\uparrow \boldsymbol{a}$. Since $\beta < 0$, $\beta\boldsymbol{a} \downarrow\uparrow \boldsymbol{a}$, and since $\alpha > 0$, $\alpha(\beta\boldsymbol{a}) \uparrow\uparrow \beta\boldsymbol{a}$. The latter vector is antiparallel to ***a***, and therefore, each of the two vectors, $(\alpha\beta)\boldsymbol{a}$ and $\alpha(\beta\boldsymbol{a})$ is antiparallel to ***a***, and hence they are parallel: $(\alpha\beta)\boldsymbol{a} \uparrow\uparrow \alpha(\beta\boldsymbol{a})$.

(iii) and (iv) should be considered by students as an exercise.

Property (7) can be proved in a similar manner: the vectors standing in the right- and left-hand sides of the equality are collinear, so the proof just requires a diligent consideration of all possible cases including α and β being positive or negative.

Let us prove the *distributive law of the addition of vectors with respect to scalar multiplication*, which is property 8. The vectors ***a*** and ***b*** mentioned in the property can be collinear or noncollinear. We shall consider here only the noncollinear case leaving the other one as an exercise.

Let ***a*** and ***b*** be some noncollinear vectors (Figure 8). ΔABC is formed by these vectors, $\overrightarrow{AB} = \boldsymbol{a}$ and $\overrightarrow{BC} = \boldsymbol{b}$, and their sum $\overrightarrow{AC} = \boldsymbol{a} + \boldsymbol{b}$. Suppose $\alpha > 0$ is some number, and let ΔMNP be formed by the $\alpha-$multiples of ***a*** and ***b***: vectors $\overrightarrow{MN} = \alpha\boldsymbol{a}$ and $\overrightarrow{NP} = \alpha\boldsymbol{b}$. Then the third side of this triangle is their sum: $\overrightarrow{MP} = \alpha\boldsymbol{a} + \alpha\boldsymbol{b}$.

Triangles ABC and MNP are similar since $\angle ABC = \angle MNP$ (as the angles with respectively parallel sides) and the sides forming these angles are in proportion: $MN : AB = NP : BC = \alpha$. Hence, the third pair of sides is in the same proportion: $MP : AC = \alpha$, or $MP = \alpha AC$. This equality can be rewritten as $\|\alpha\overrightarrow{AB} + \alpha\overrightarrow{BC}\| = \alpha\|\overrightarrow{AB} + \overrightarrow{BC}\|$, or $\|\alpha\boldsymbol{a} + \alpha\boldsymbol{b}\| = \alpha\|\boldsymbol{a} + \boldsymbol{b}\|$. Also, due to the similarity of the triangles, $\angle CAB = \angle PMN$, which implies $MP \parallel AC$. The latter means the collinearity of $\overrightarrow{MP}$ and $\overrightarrow{AC}$, i.e. the vectors $\alpha\boldsymbol{a} + \alpha\boldsymbol{b}$ and $\alpha(\boldsymbol{a} + \boldsymbol{b})$ are collinear.

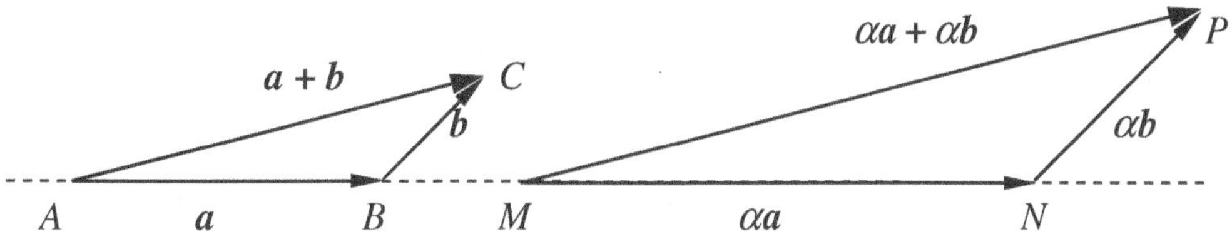

Figure 8

It is easy to see that these vectors are parallel (co-directed) if $\alpha > 0$. For instance, one can perform such a simultaneous parallel translation of the vectors forming ΔMNP that $\alpha \boldsymbol{a}$ lies on the same line as $\boldsymbol{a}$ (the dotted line in the figure). Then, if $\alpha > 0$, the terminal points of $\boldsymbol{b}$ and $\alpha \boldsymbol{b}$ will lie on the same side from this line. (Similarly, they will lie on the opposite sides of this line if $\alpha < 0$.) Thus, it has been proved that the vectors $\alpha \boldsymbol{a} + \alpha \boldsymbol{b}$ and $\alpha(\boldsymbol{a} + \boldsymbol{b})$ are parallel, and their norms are equal, therefore the vectors are equal if α is positive. The case of negative α can be considered in a similar manner with minor adjustments.

This completes the last proof of the basic properties of linear operations with geometric vectors. Let us list these properties again:

(1) For any vectors $\boldsymbol{a}$ and $\boldsymbol{b}$, $\boldsymbol{a} + \boldsymbol{b} = \boldsymbol{b} + \boldsymbol{a}$ *(commutative law of addition).*

(2) For any vectors $\boldsymbol{a}$, $\boldsymbol{b}$, and $\boldsymbol{c}$, $\boldsymbol{a} + (\boldsymbol{b} + \boldsymbol{c}) = (\boldsymbol{a} + \boldsymbol{b}) + \boldsymbol{c}$ *(associative law of addition).*

(3) For any vector $\boldsymbol{a}$, $\boldsymbol{a} + \boldsymbol{0} = \boldsymbol{a}$ *(the existence of zero).*

(4) For any vector $\boldsymbol{a}$, there exists such a vector $-\boldsymbol{a}$, that $\boldsymbol{a} + (-\boldsymbol{a}) = \boldsymbol{0}$ *(the existence of the opposite, or additive inverse).*

(5) For any vector $\boldsymbol{a}$, $1 \cdot \boldsymbol{a} = \boldsymbol{a}$ *(scaling property).*

(6) For any vector $\boldsymbol{a}$ and any numbers α, β, $(\alpha\beta)\boldsymbol{a} = \alpha(\beta \boldsymbol{a})$ *(associative law).*

(7) For any vector $\boldsymbol{a}$ and any numbers α, β, $(\alpha + \beta)\boldsymbol{a} = \alpha \boldsymbol{a} + \beta \boldsymbol{a}$ *(distributive law).*

(8) For any vectors $\boldsymbol{a}$ and $\boldsymbol{b}$ and any number α, $\alpha(\boldsymbol{a} + \boldsymbol{b}) = \alpha \boldsymbol{a} + \alpha \boldsymbol{b}$ *(distributive law).*

These properties are of crucial importance for our subject since they are assumed to be the defining properties of linear operations for *any kind of vectors*, not only the geometric ones.

1.3 LINEAR COMBINATIONS OF VECTORS. LINEAR INDEPENDENCE. SPANNING SETS.

Definition. Let $\boldsymbol{e}_1, \boldsymbol{e}_2, \ldots, \boldsymbol{e}_n$ be a few vectors. A vector made out of these vectors by means of linear operations, i.e. any vector $\boldsymbol{a}$ of the form

$$\boldsymbol{a} = \alpha_1 \boldsymbol{e}_1 + \alpha_2 \boldsymbol{e}_2 + \ldots + \alpha_n \boldsymbol{e}_n ,$$

is called a *linear combination* of these vectors. The numbers $\alpha_1, \alpha_2, \ldots, \alpha_n$ are said to be the coefficients of the linear combination.

It follows from the definition that a linear combination of a single vector is just a scalar multiple of this vector.

Example 1. Vector $\boldsymbol{a} = 3\boldsymbol{b} + 2c - 5\boldsymbol{d}$ is a linear combination of $\boldsymbol{b}$, $\boldsymbol{c}$, and $\boldsymbol{d}$ with the coefficients 3, 2, and -5.

Example 2. Let vectors $\boldsymbol{m}$ and $\boldsymbol{n}$ originate at the same point O. In a parallelogram constructed on these vectors as its sides, each diagonal is a linear combination of $\boldsymbol{m}$ and $\boldsymbol{n}$: the diagonal that emanates from O is $\boldsymbol{m} + \boldsymbol{n}$, whereas the other diagonal is either $\boldsymbol{m} - \boldsymbol{n}$ or $\boldsymbol{n} - \boldsymbol{m}$.

Example 3. If there exist such scalars (numbers) α and β that $\boldsymbol{a} = \alpha\boldsymbol{u} + \beta\boldsymbol{v}$, then $\boldsymbol{a}$ is a linear combination of $\boldsymbol{u}$ and $\boldsymbol{v}$ with the coefficients α and β.

Also, we can use the properties of linear operations to rewrite the above equality as $\boldsymbol{a} - \alpha\boldsymbol{u} - \beta\boldsymbol{v} = \boldsymbol{0}$, which means that $\boldsymbol{0}$ is a linear combination of $\boldsymbol{a}$, $\boldsymbol{u}$, and $\boldsymbol{v}$. Later in this course we shall call such vectors as $\boldsymbol{a}$, $\boldsymbol{u}$, and $\boldsymbol{v}$ *linearly dependent*. They have deserved this special name since their linear combination with non-zero coefficients (at least the first coefficient is 1, not 0) is a zero vector. *Linearly dependent* sets of vectors play an important role in linear algebra.

Example 4. In Figure 1, where $AB = BC = CD = DE$, each of the vectors $\overrightarrow{AE}, \overrightarrow{AB}, \overrightarrow{DC}, \overrightarrow{DA}$ is a multiple and therefore a linear combination of $\overrightarrow{AC}$:
$\overrightarrow{AE} = 2\overrightarrow{AC}$; $\overrightarrow{AB} = \frac{1}{2}\overrightarrow{AC}$; $\overrightarrow{DC} = -\frac{1}{2}\overrightarrow{AC}$; $\overrightarrow{DA} = -\frac{3}{2}\overrightarrow{AC}$.

Each time, in order to create a required linear combination, we had to multiply $\overrightarrow{AC}$ by a factor that would adjust its length. This factor is positive if the considered vector is co-directed with $\overrightarrow{AC}$ and negative otherwise. Thus, the factor is completely determined (mathematicians say: *uniquely defined*) by the vector that is to be obtained as a multiple of $\overrightarrow{AC}$. If, for instance, we multiply $\overrightarrow{AC}$ by some other number than 2, we will never obtain $\overrightarrow{AE}$.

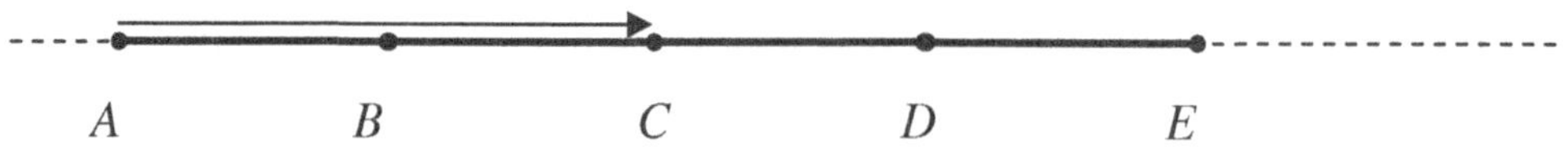

Figure 1

It is quite clear from this consideration that any vector lying in the same line as $\overrightarrow{AC}$ is its multiple, i.e. its linear combination. Let us formulate and prove this result *in general*.

Theorem 1.3.1 Any vector $\boldsymbol{a}$ collinear with a nonzero vector $\boldsymbol{e}$ is its linear combination, i.e. for any vector $\boldsymbol{a}$ collinear with a given nonzero vector $\boldsymbol{e}$, there exists such a scalar α that $\boldsymbol{a} = \alpha\boldsymbol{e}$. This number α is *uniquely defined* for every $\boldsymbol{a}$.

Proof At first we shall proof the existence of α, and then its uniqueness.

Let us choose $\alpha = \frac{\|\boldsymbol{a}\|}{\|\boldsymbol{e}\|}$ if $\boldsymbol{a}$ is co-directed with $\boldsymbol{e}$, and $\alpha = -\frac{\|\boldsymbol{a}\|}{\|\boldsymbol{e}\|}$ if these two vectors are oppositely directed. Then:

(1) the obtained vector $\alpha\boldsymbol{e}$ is co-directed with $\boldsymbol{e}$ if $\boldsymbol{a}$ is co-directed and directed oppositely to $\boldsymbol{e}$ if $\boldsymbol{a}$ is directed oppositely to $\boldsymbol{e}$, which means the direction of $\alpha\boldsymbol{e}$ is the same as the direction of $\boldsymbol{a}$;

(2) in any of these cases, the norm of $\alpha\boldsymbol{e}$ is $\|\alpha\boldsymbol{e}\| = |\alpha| \cdot \|\boldsymbol{e}\| = \frac{\|\boldsymbol{a}\|}{\|\boldsymbol{e}\|}\|\boldsymbol{e}\| = \|\boldsymbol{a}\|$, i.e. the length of $\alpha\boldsymbol{e}$ is the same as that of $\boldsymbol{a}$.

Therefore, the proposed α is such that $\boldsymbol{a} = \alpha\boldsymbol{e}$ for any vector $\boldsymbol{a}$ collinear with $\boldsymbol{e}$.

Now let us prove that α is *defined uniquely*, i.e. if $\boldsymbol{a} = \alpha\boldsymbol{e}$ and $\boldsymbol{a} = \beta\boldsymbol{e}$, then $\beta = \alpha$.

Since $\beta\boldsymbol{e} = \alpha\boldsymbol{e}$, the norms of these vectors are equal:

$\|\beta\boldsymbol{e}\| = \|\alpha\boldsymbol{e}\|; \Rightarrow |\beta| \cdot \|\boldsymbol{e}\| = |\alpha| \cdot \|\boldsymbol{e}\|; \Rightarrow |\beta| = |\alpha|$. Also, α and β cannot have opposite signs since the vectors $\beta\boldsymbol{e}$ and $\alpha\boldsymbol{e}$ are equal and therefore co-directed.

The proof of the theorem is complete. □

Remark. Let us notice that, in the conditions of the above theorem, not only the number α is *uniquely defined* for every $\boldsymbol{a}$, but also the *converse* is true: each vector $\boldsymbol{a}$ is uniquely defined by a number α such that $\boldsymbol{a} = \alpha\boldsymbol{e}$. Really, if $\alpha = \beta$, then the norms of the vectors $\boldsymbol{a} = \alpha\boldsymbol{e}$ and $\boldsymbol{b} = \beta\boldsymbol{e}$ will be equal:

$\|\boldsymbol{a}\| = \|\alpha\boldsymbol{e}\| = |\alpha| \cdot \|\boldsymbol{e}\| = |\beta| \cdot \|\boldsymbol{e}\| = \|\beta\boldsymbol{e}\| = \|\boldsymbol{b}\|$,

and since equal numbers have the same sign, these vectors will be co-directed; thus $\alpha\boldsymbol{e} = \beta\boldsymbol{e}$ if $\alpha = \beta$.

Since this almost obvious fact has very important consequences (it will allow us to introduce coordinate axes), we shall formulate it as a separate statement, called a corollary (by this word we denote all statements that follow directly from others).

Corollary 1. Given a nonzero vector $\boldsymbol{e}$, there is a *one-to-one correspondence* between the vectors collinear with $\boldsymbol{e}$ and the real numbers: for every number α there is exactly one vector $\boldsymbol{a} = \alpha\boldsymbol{e}$, and for every vector $\boldsymbol{a}$ collinear with $\boldsymbol{e}$ there is exactly one number α such that $\alpha\boldsymbol{e} = \boldsymbol{a}$.

We denote this correspondence by $\boldsymbol{a} \leftrightarrow \alpha$.

We shall soon return to this correspondence in order to introduce coordinate systems. In the meantime we shall consider some other important notions that will enable us to generalize the results of Theorem1 for various sets of vectors. These notions are those of *linear independence* and *spanning sets*.

It follows from Theorem1 that, given two collinear vectors, we can make their linear combination $\boldsymbol{0}$ (a vector) without multiplying each of them by 0 (the number). Really, the equality $\boldsymbol{a} = \alpha\boldsymbol{e}$ can be rewritten as $\boldsymbol{a} - \alpha\boldsymbol{e} = \boldsymbol{0}$. This means that a linear combination of $\boldsymbol{a}$ and $\boldsymbol{e}$ is $\boldsymbol{0}$ and at least one of the coefficients, the coefficient with $\boldsymbol{a}$, is non-zero (it is equal to 1).

We have already seen similar situations. In Example1 of the previous subsection we wrote $\boldsymbol{v}+\boldsymbol{a}+(-\boldsymbol{b})+\boldsymbol{c}+(-\boldsymbol{d})+(-\boldsymbol{e})=\boldsymbol{0}$, which means that a linear combination of the vectors $\boldsymbol{v},\boldsymbol{a},\boldsymbol{b},\boldsymbol{c},\boldsymbol{d}$, and $\boldsymbol{e}$ with the respective coefficients 1, 1, –1, 1, –1, and –1, is a zero vector.

At the same time, some sets of vectors do not have such a property. For instance, *a linear combination of two noncollinear vectors is* $\boldsymbol{0}$ *only in the case when each coefficient of the combination is* 0.

Really, let $\boldsymbol{a}$ and $\boldsymbol{b}$ be two noncollinear vectors. Suppose their linear combination with coefficients α and β is a zero vector and at least one of the coefficients is not zero: $\alpha\boldsymbol{a} + \beta\boldsymbol{b} = \boldsymbol{0}$, and $\alpha \neq 0$. Then we can rewrite the relation between $\boldsymbol{a}$ and $\boldsymbol{b}$ as $\alpha\boldsymbol{a} = -\beta\boldsymbol{b}$, and since $\alpha \neq 0$, we can multiply the last equality by $\frac{1}{\alpha}$. Then $\boldsymbol{a} = -\frac{\beta}{\alpha}\boldsymbol{b}$. This equality means that $\boldsymbol{a}$ is a multiple of $\boldsymbol{b}$, which is impossible since they are noncollinear. Thus we have arrived to a contradiction, which shows that our assumption that $\alpha \neq 0$ is false. Therefore, $\alpha = 0$. Similarly, we can show that $\beta = 0$.

Hence, $\alpha\boldsymbol{a} + \beta\boldsymbol{b} = \boldsymbol{0}$ only if each of the coefficients is 0.

Definition. A set of vectors $\boldsymbol{e}_1,\boldsymbol{e}_2,\ldots,\boldsymbol{e}_n$ is called *linearly independent* if a linear combination of these vectors is equal to a zero vector only when each coefficient of the combination is zero. Otherwise (if a linear combination of the vectors of a set is $\boldsymbol{0}$ and at least one coefficient is not 0) the set is called *linearly dependent.*

Example 5. The set of vectors $\boldsymbol{v},\boldsymbol{a},\boldsymbol{b},\boldsymbol{c},\boldsymbol{d}$, and $\boldsymbol{e}$ of Example1 of the previous subsection is linearly dependent.

Example 6. Let $\boldsymbol{m}$ and $\boldsymbol{n}$ be some vectors, and $\boldsymbol{p} = 3\boldsymbol{m} + 4\boldsymbol{n}$. Then the set $\boldsymbol{m}$, $\boldsymbol{n}$, and $\boldsymbol{p}$ is linearly dependent. Really, it is easy to compose a $\boldsymbol{0}$ linear combination of these vectors without multiplying all of them by 0: $3\boldsymbol{m} + 4\boldsymbol{n} - \boldsymbol{p} = \boldsymbol{0}$.

The results of our discussion preceding the definition of linear dependence can be formulated as a proposition (a proven statement):

Proposition 1. Two geometric vectors are linearly dependent if and only if they are collinear.

There are a few more important propositions that are easy to prove (try to do this!).

Proposition 2. Any set of vectors that contains a zero vector is linearly dependent.

Proposition 3. Any set of vectors that contains a linearly dependent subset is linearly dependent.

Proposition 4. A set of vectors is linearly dependent if and only if one of them is a linear combination of the others.

It should be noticed that the latter proposition contains two statements that are to be proved:

(i) A set of vectors is linearly dependent if one of them is a linear combination of the others.

(ii) If a set of vectors is linearly dependent, then (at least) one of the vectors of the set is a linear combination of the others.

The proof of this proposition is analogous to our discussion of the linear dependence between two collinear vectors or independence between two noncollinear ones.

Definition. The set of all linear combinations of a given set of vectors is called the *spanning set* (or just *span*) of these vectors. Thus we say that some vector $\boldsymbol{v}$ belongs to the spannning set of $\{\boldsymbol{e}_1, \boldsymbol{e}_2, \ldots, \boldsymbol{e}_n\}$ and we write $\boldsymbol{v} \in Span\{\boldsymbol{e}_1, \boldsymbol{e}_2, \ldots, \boldsymbol{e}_n\}$ if $\boldsymbol{v}$ is a linear combination of $\{\boldsymbol{e}_1, \boldsymbol{e}_2, \ldots, \boldsymbol{e}_n\}$, i.e. if there exist such scalars $\alpha_1, \alpha_2, \ldots, \alpha_n$ that $\boldsymbol{v} = \alpha_1 \boldsymbol{e}_1 + \alpha_2 \boldsymbol{e}_2 + \ldots + \alpha_n \boldsymbol{e}_n$.

In other words, a vector is in the spanning set of a few vectors if it can be presented as their linear combination.

In case of a single vector, the spanning set of this vector is the set of all its multiples. If a vector is not zero, then, according to Theorem 1, the spanning set of a vector consists of all vectors that are collinear with it. Such a set is called the *line of vectors* collinear with the given vectors.

Also, it follows from the definition of a scalar multiple of a vector that *a vector does not span any vectors that are noncollinear with it.* Let us prove this statement *by contradiction.* (That means: we suggest the opposite of what we are trying to prove, and because of this suggestion we shall arrive to a contradiction. Thus we shall see that our suggestion has been false). Suppose $\boldsymbol{b}$ is not collinear with $\boldsymbol{e}$, and still $\boldsymbol{b} \in Span\{\boldsymbol{e}\}$. The latter means that there exists such a number β that $\boldsymbol{b} = \beta \boldsymbol{e}$, and therefore, by definition of scalar multiplication, $\boldsymbol{b}$ is collinear with $\boldsymbol{e}$, which is impossible. The obtained contradiction shows that $\boldsymbol{b} \notin Span\{\boldsymbol{e}\}$.

This statement together with the results of Theorem 1 can be formulated as another theorem.

Theorem 1.3.2 A non-zero vector $\boldsymbol{e}$ spans the set of all vectors (the *line of vectors*) collinear with it, and only vectors from this line (collinear with it) are in its spanning set.

Example 7. Let in Figure 2 $\overrightarrow{CA} = \boldsymbol{v}$, and $\overrightarrow{OD} = \boldsymbol{e}$. Let us present some other vector collinear with them, for instance vector $\overrightarrow{OF}$, as their linear combination. It turns out we can do this in a few different ways. For example, $\overrightarrow{OF} = 3\boldsymbol{e}$; also $\overrightarrow{OF} = -\frac{3}{2}\boldsymbol{v}$; $\overrightarrow{OF} = 5\boldsymbol{e} + \boldsymbol{v}$; $\overrightarrow{OF} = 2\boldsymbol{e} - \frac{1}{2}\boldsymbol{v}$; etc.

It is clear that we can continue this list forever, i.e. vector $\overrightarrow{OF}$ can be presented as a linear combination of $\boldsymbol{e}$ and $\boldsymbol{v}$ in many (actually, infinitely many) different ways. In other words, the coefficients of such a linear combination are *not defined uniquely.*

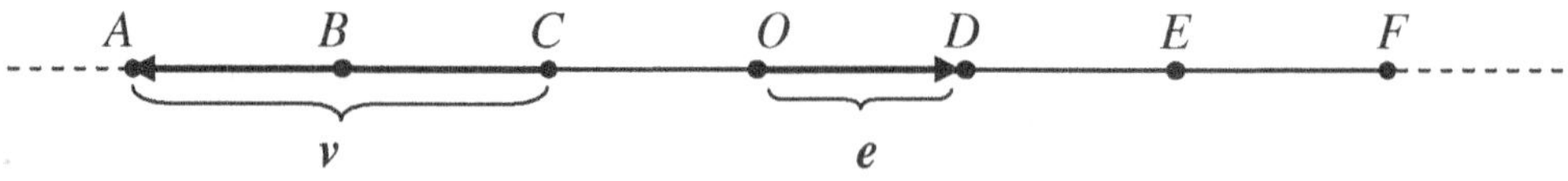

Figure 2

(If, however, we exclude one of the vectors $\boldsymbol{e}$ or $\boldsymbol{v}$ from the above expressions, we shall obtain a uniquely defined expression, as is expected according to Corollary 1. For instance, by substituting $\boldsymbol{v} = -2\boldsymbol{e}$ in any of the three expressions, we shall get $\overrightarrow{OF} = 3\boldsymbol{e}$).

It is easy to show (try to do this) that the statement of Example 7 is true in general: given two (or more) collinear vectors, any vector collinear with them is their linear combination, and the coefficients of such a combination are *not uniquely defined*, in contrast with the case considered in Theorem 1 when a single vector spans the line.

Thus, a single nonzero vector has a very special role in the set of all vectors collinear with it: it spans every vector of the set in a uniquely defined way. Because of this property, it deserves a special name: it is called a *basis* in the line.

It will be shown later on in the course that every vector space has a *basis – such a set of vectors that every vector from the space is their linear combination, and this linear combination is defined uniquely.* The reason for this uniqueness lies in the *linear independence* of the vectors that constitute a basis. After considering a few specific examples of bases, a general definition will be given: we shall define a *basis in a space of vectors as a linearly independent set of vectors that span every vector of the space.*

The meaning of the latter paragraph will be clearer after the next section, in which we shall consider the notion of basis for various types of sets of geometric vectors: line, plane, and space.

1.4 A BASIS IN A LINE, IN A PLANE, AND IN SPACE OF GEOMETRIC VECTORS. COORDINATE SYSTEMS AND SPACES R, R^2, AND R^3.

(i) A line of vectors and *R*.

As it has been established in Theorem 1(section 1.3), a nonzero vector spans the whole line of vectors collinear with it, and every vector in the line is uniquely defined as its multiple. This result enables us to give the following definition.

Definition. A *basis in a line of vectors* is any nonzero vector $\boldsymbol{e}$ from this line. If $\boldsymbol{a} = \alpha\boldsymbol{e}$, then α is called the *coordinate* (or *component*) of $\boldsymbol{a}$ in the basis $\{\boldsymbol{e}\}$.

It is obvious that a set consisting of a single nonzero vector $\boldsymbol{e}$ is linearly independent: we cannot make a multiple of this vector $\boldsymbol{0}$ unless we multiply it by 0: $\alpha\boldsymbol{e} = \boldsymbol{0}$ if and only if $\alpha = 0$. Really, $\|0 \cdot \boldsymbol{e}\| = 0 \cdot \|\boldsymbol{e}\| = 0$, so $0 \cdot \boldsymbol{e}$ is a zero vector, whereas if $\alpha \neq 0$, $\|\alpha\boldsymbol{e}\| = \|\alpha\| \cdot \|\boldsymbol{e}\| \neq 0$, so $\alpha\boldsymbol{e}$ is not a zero vector.

The existence of a basis in a line allows us to turn a line into a so-called *coordinate axis*. Let l be a line and $\boldsymbol{e} \neq \boldsymbol{0}$ a vector collinear with this line, i.e. $\boldsymbol{e}$ lies on l or on a line parallel to l. Let O be a point lying on this line. Let us translate vector $\boldsymbol{e}$ so that its origin is located at O. We shall call point O the *origin* of the coordinate axis and assign this point an *affine coordinate* of 0.Then the terminal point of $\boldsymbol{e}$ will be located at some point E of the line. We shall assign this point an *affine coordinate* of 1. (For brevity, we shall often say *coordinate* instead of *affine coordinate*).

We have created a *coordinate axis*: a straight line with the origin O and a basis vector $\boldsymbol{e}$, which determines the *positive direction* and the *scale unit* on the axis (Figure 1).

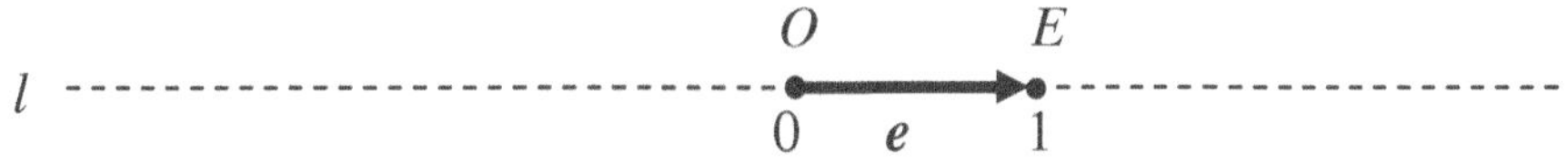

Figure 1

Now, every point A of this axis can be joined with the origin by means of a vector $\boldsymbol{a} = \overrightarrow{OA}$, emanating from the origin O and ending at A. According to Theorem1 and its corollary, there exists one and only one number α such that $\boldsymbol{a} = \alpha\boldsymbol{e}$. We shall call this number α the *affine coordinate* of point A, and vector $\boldsymbol{a} = \overrightarrow{OA}$ will be called the *position vector* of this point. (The origin of this term is clear: the position of every point of the axis and thus its coordinate is uniquely defined by the vector joining the origin of the axis with this point). Let us notice that, in contrast with the so-called *free vectors* which can be translated, *position vectors* always start from the origin.

By assigning each point its position vector we have established a one-to-one correspondence between the points of the line and real numbers: $A \leftrightarrow \alpha$ if

$\overrightarrow{OA} = \alpha \boldsymbol{e} \leftrightarrow \alpha$. The affine coordinate of each point (A) is presented by the same number (α) as the coordinate of the position vector $\boldsymbol{a} = \overrightarrow{OA}$ in the basis $\{\boldsymbol{e}\}$. Thus we have established a one-to-one correspondence between the set V^1 of all vectors collinear with $\boldsymbol{e}$ and originating at O and the set R of all real numbers: $V^1 \leftrightarrow R$ determined by the correspondence $\overrightarrow{OA} = \boldsymbol{a} = \alpha \boldsymbol{e} \leftrightarrow \alpha$.

Moreover, we shall illustrate on examples and then prove that this correspondence is *preserved by linear operations*: if vectors are added, then their coordinates are to be added, and if a vector is multiplied by a number, its coordinate is to be multiplied by the same number. We can write this symbolically as:

$$\left.\begin{array}{l} \boldsymbol{a} \leftrightarrow \alpha \\ \boldsymbol{b} \leftrightarrow \beta \end{array}\right\} \Rightarrow \left\{\begin{array}{c} \boldsymbol{a}+\boldsymbol{b} \leftrightarrow \alpha+\beta \\ \text{and} \\ k\boldsymbol{a} \leftrightarrow k\alpha \end{array}\right.$$

Example 1. In Figure 2, showing a coordinate axis with $\boldsymbol{e}$ as a basis vector and origin O, the affine coordinates of some points can be determined as follows:
Coordinate of point A is -3, since $\boldsymbol{a} = \overrightarrow{OA} = (-3)\boldsymbol{e}$.

Coordinate of point D is 2, since $\overrightarrow{OD} = 2\boldsymbol{e}$.
Coordinate of point B is -2, since $\overrightarrow{OB} = (-2)\boldsymbol{e}$.

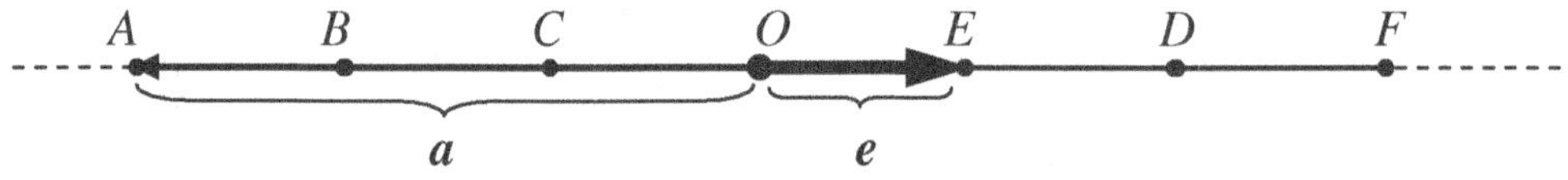

Figure 2

Let us notice that the coordinate of point B in the last example could also be determined by the following calculation:

$$\overrightarrow{OB} = \overrightarrow{OA} + \overrightarrow{OE} = \boldsymbol{a} + \boldsymbol{e} = (-3)\boldsymbol{e} + \boldsymbol{e} = (-2)\boldsymbol{e}.$$

At the same time

(coordinate of A) + (coordinate of E) = $-3 + 1 = -2$ = (coordinate of B).

Here is what we have observed: $\boldsymbol{a} \leftrightarrow (-3)$, $\boldsymbol{e} \leftrightarrow 1$, and $\boldsymbol{a}+\boldsymbol{e} \leftrightarrow (-3)+1$.

Thus we have illustrated (not proved yet!) that the correspondence is preserved under addition:

If the position vector of a point is a sum of two vectors, then the coordinate of this point is the sum of the coordinates of these two vectors:

$$\left.\begin{array}{l} \boldsymbol{a} \leftrightarrow \alpha \\ \boldsymbol{b} \leftrightarrow \beta \end{array}\right\} \Rightarrow \boldsymbol{a}+\boldsymbol{b} \leftrightarrow \alpha+\beta \qquad (1)$$

Now let us look at an example showing that the correspondence is preserved under multiplication by numbers:

$\overrightarrow{OF} = \left(-\frac{3}{2}\right)\overrightarrow{OB} = \left(-\frac{3}{2}\right)(-2)\boldsymbol{e} = 3\boldsymbol{e}$, so the coordinate of F is equal to 3,

and

$\left(-\frac{3}{2}\right)$ (coordinate of B) = $\left(-\frac{3}{2}\right)(-2) = 2$ = (coordinate of F).

This illustrates the preservation of the correspondence under scalar multiplication: *If the position vector of a point is a multiple of some vector, then the coordinate of the point is a multiple of the coordinate of the same vector with the same coefficient*:

$$\boldsymbol{a} \leftrightarrow \alpha \quad \Rightarrow \quad k\boldsymbol{a} \leftrightarrow k\alpha \tag{2}$$

One can use the properties of linear operations to show that such relations between the coordinates of the points and their position vectors hold in general and thus the following theorem follows:

Theorem 1.4.1 Let P be some point on the coordinate axis with the origin O and basis $\{\boldsymbol{e}\}$. If the position vector $\overrightarrow{OP}$ of point P is a linear combination of two vectors, with some coefficients, then the affine coordinate of P is a linear combination of the coordinates of these vectors with the same coefficients.

In other words, if $\overrightarrow{OP} = k_1\boldsymbol{a} + k_2\boldsymbol{b}$, where $\boldsymbol{a} = \alpha\boldsymbol{e}$ and $\boldsymbol{b} = \beta\boldsymbol{e}$, then the affine coordinate of point P is $k_1\alpha + k_2\beta$.

We can briefly express this property by saying that the established correspondence between V^1 and R is preserved under linear operations:

$$\left.\begin{array}{l} \boldsymbol{a} \leftrightarrow \alpha \\ \boldsymbol{b} \leftrightarrow \beta \end{array}\right\} \Rightarrow \left(k_1\boldsymbol{a} + k_2\boldsymbol{b}\right) \leftrightarrow \left(k_1\alpha + k_2\beta\right) \tag{3}$$

(It is easy to show that condition (3) is equivalent to (1) and (2) together).

Such a correspondence is called an *isomorphism* (having the same form) and it means that the two sets (in our case V^1 and R) are not different from the point of view of linear algebra, even though the objects constituting these sets are of different nature (vectors for V^1 and numbers for R).

The correspondence between the affine coordinates of points and the coordinates of their position vectors can be used to find the coordinates of vectors connecting various points.

For instance, one can find for $\overrightarrow{CF}$ in Figure 2:

$\overrightarrow{CF} = \overrightarrow{OF} - \overrightarrow{OC} = 3\boldsymbol{e} - (-1)\boldsymbol{e} = \left(3-(-1)\right)\boldsymbol{e} = \left(\text{coordinate of } F - \text{coordinate of } C\right)\boldsymbol{e} = 4\boldsymbol{e}$

We can show that this result is true in general: *in order to find the coordinate of a vector joining two points on a coordinate axis, one should subtract the coordinate of the origin (tail) of the vector from the coordinate of its terminal point.*
Since it is of great practical importance, we shall formulate it as a theorem:

Theorem 1.4.2 If A and B are two points on a coordinate axis, and their respective coordinates are x_A and x_B, then the coordinate of the vector $\overrightarrow{AB}$ connecting these points is $x_B - x_A$.

Proof. This result follows immediately from Theorem 1. It can also be proved as follows.

Let O be the origin of the coordinate axis on which A and B are located and $\boldsymbol{e}$ be a basis on this axis. We shall find the coordinate of $\overrightarrow{AB}$ in this basis.

$$\overrightarrow{AB} = \overrightarrow{OB} - \overrightarrow{OA} = x_B\boldsymbol{e} - x_A\boldsymbol{e} = (x_B - x_A)\boldsymbol{e}, \tag{4}$$

which proves the statement. □

(ii) A plane of vectors and R^2.

Now let us discuss the sets of vectors that lie in the same plane or can be brought in the same plane by means of parallel translations; we shall call such vectors *coplanar*. The set of all vectors that are coplanar with each other will be called *a plane of vectors*.

One of the axioms of Euclidean geometry asserts that there is exactly one plane that contains two given intersecting lines. Therefore *two vectors are always coplanar*: their origins can be made to coincide by a parallel translation, and each of them determines a straight line. Three or more vectors may be *noncoplanar*.

Concerning a plane of vectors, we will be interested in the same kind of questions that we posed for a line of vectors: How many vectors are needed to span a plane? What are the conditions of linear independence of vectors in a plane? Can we create a planar coordinate system?

Let us start with some simple examples.

Example 2. In Figure 3 below, $ABEF$ and $BCDE$ are squares, and the points M and N are the midpoints of the sides FA and CD respectively. $\overrightarrow{MA} = \boldsymbol{u}$; $\overrightarrow{FB} = \boldsymbol{v}$.
Express the following vectors as linear combinations of $\boldsymbol{u}$ and $\boldsymbol{v}$:
(i) $\overrightarrow{AE}$; (ii) $\overrightarrow{FN}$; (iii) $\overrightarrow{FC}$.

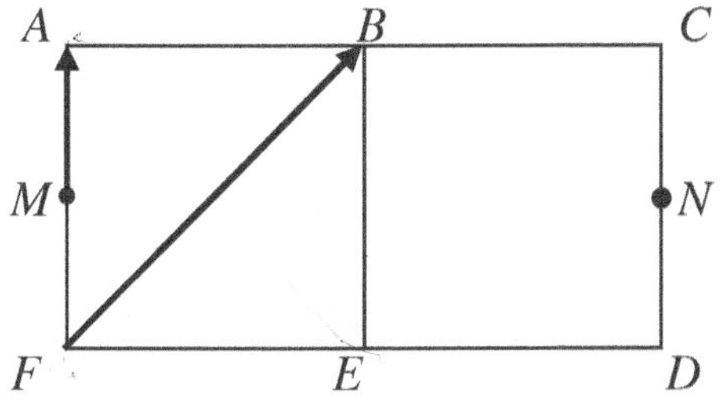

Figure 3

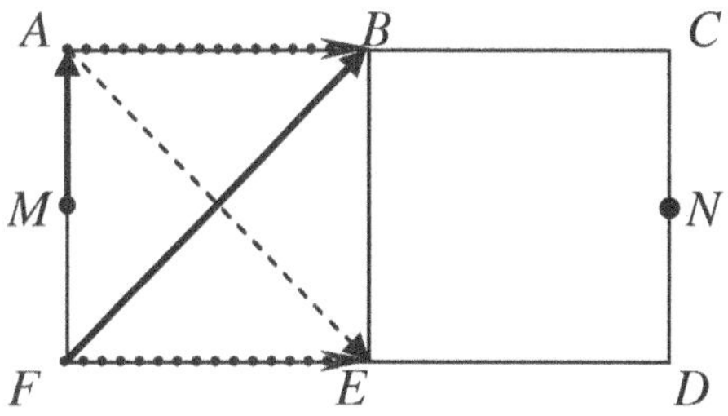

Figure 4

<u>Solution.</u> (i) $\overrightarrow{AE}$ can be viewed as the difference between $\overrightarrow{FE}$ and $\overrightarrow{FA}$, since (see Figure 6) $\overrightarrow{FA}+\overrightarrow{AE}=\overrightarrow{FE}$. Therefore, $\overrightarrow{AE}=\overrightarrow{FE}-\overrightarrow{FA}=\overrightarrow{FE}-2\boldsymbol{u}$. Now we have to express $\overrightarrow{FE}$ through $\boldsymbol{u}$ and $\boldsymbol{v}$.

Since *FE* and *AB* are the opposite sides of a square, their lengths are equal and they are parallel, hence $\overrightarrow{FE}=\overrightarrow{AB}$. From triangle *FAB*, one can see that $\overrightarrow{FA}+\overrightarrow{AB}=\overrightarrow{FB}$, whence $\overrightarrow{AB}=\overrightarrow{FB}-\overrightarrow{FA}=\boldsymbol{v}-2\boldsymbol{u}$. Thus, $\overrightarrow{FE}=\overrightarrow{AB}=\boldsymbol{v}-2\boldsymbol{u}$, and after substituting this expression into $\overrightarrow{AE}=\overrightarrow{FE}-2\boldsymbol{u}$, we obtain
$\overrightarrow{AE}=(\boldsymbol{v}-2\boldsymbol{u})-2\boldsymbol{u}=\boldsymbol{v}-4\boldsymbol{u}$.

Answer: $\overrightarrow{AE}=-4\boldsymbol{u}+\boldsymbol{v}$, i.e. $\overrightarrow{AE}$ is a linear combination of $\boldsymbol{u}$ and $\boldsymbol{v}$ with the coefficients -4 and 1.

(ii) $\overrightarrow{FN}$ can be viewed as the sum of $\overrightarrow{FD}$ and $\overrightarrow{DN}$ (Figure 5); then
$\overrightarrow{FN}=\overrightarrow{FD}+\overrightarrow{DN}=2\overrightarrow{FE}+\overrightarrow{MA}=2(\boldsymbol{v}-2\boldsymbol{u})+\boldsymbol{u}=2\boldsymbol{v}-4\boldsymbol{u}+\boldsymbol{u}=-3\boldsymbol{u}+2\boldsymbol{v}$.

The same result will be obtained if we consider $\overrightarrow{FN}$ as the sum of $\overrightarrow{FO}$ and $\overrightarrow{ON}$ (where *O* is the midpoint of *FB* in Figure 5):
$\overrightarrow{FN}=\overrightarrow{FO}+\overrightarrow{ON}=\frac{1}{2}\overrightarrow{FB}+\frac{3}{2}\overrightarrow{AB}=\frac{1}{2}\boldsymbol{v}+\frac{3}{2}(\boldsymbol{v}-2\boldsymbol{u})=\frac{1}{2}\boldsymbol{v}+\frac{3}{2}\boldsymbol{v}-3\boldsymbol{u}=-3\boldsymbol{u}+2\boldsymbol{v}$.

Answer: $\overrightarrow{FN}=-3\boldsymbol{u}+2\boldsymbol{v}$.

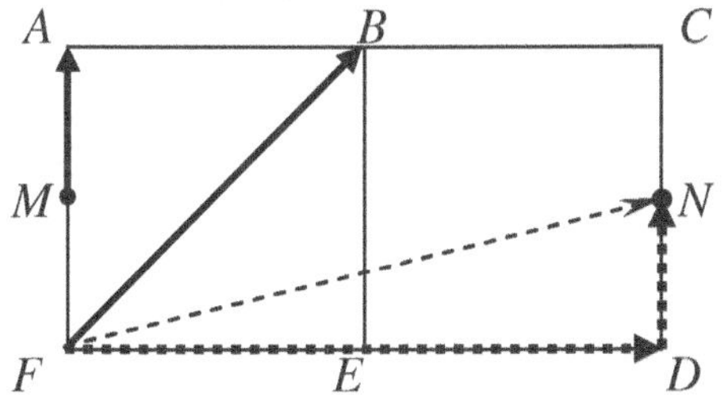

Figure 5

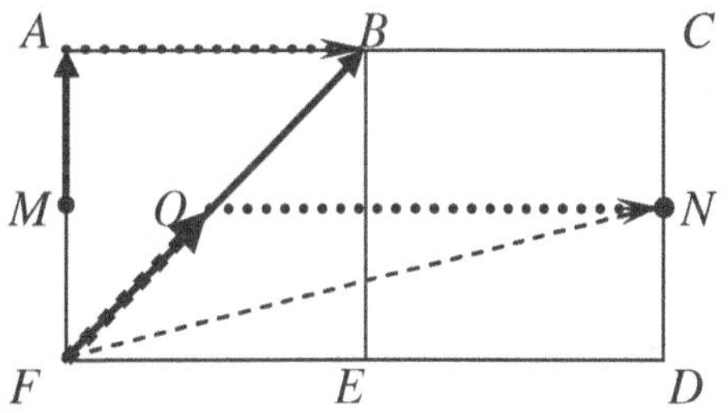

Figure 6

(iii) One of many possible solutions (see Figure 7):
$\overrightarrow{FC}=\overrightarrow{FB}+\overrightarrow{BC}=\boldsymbol{v}+(\boldsymbol{v}-2\boldsymbol{u})=2\boldsymbol{v}-2\boldsymbol{u}=-2\boldsymbol{u}+2\boldsymbol{v}$.

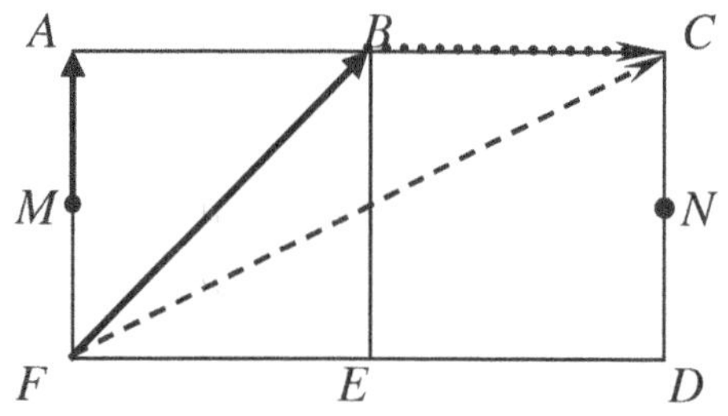

Figure 7

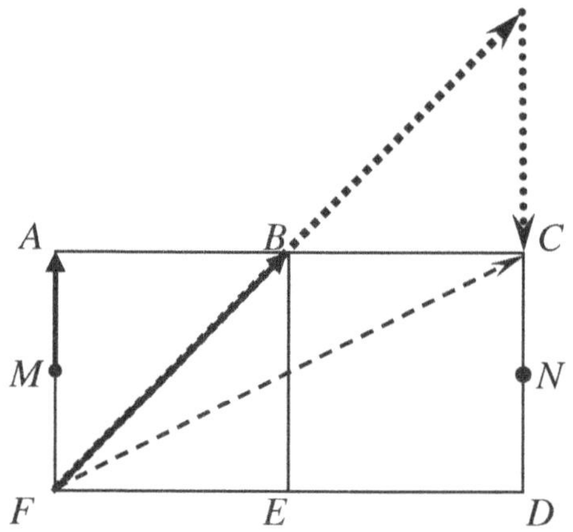

Figure 8

The same result can be obtained in one step from Figure 8, where the diagram presents the required vector (in this case $\overrightarrow{FC}$) as a sum of multiples of given vectors ($\boldsymbol{u}$ and $\boldsymbol{v}$). Therefore Figure 8 provides an illustration to a better solution. Moreover, the idea of this solution, in contrast with the others presented above, is in some sense *universal*: it can be used, as we will show shortly, for any problem of this kind, when it is solvable, of course. (Draw diagrams for one-step solutions for the other two cases: (i) to find $\overrightarrow{AE}$, and (ii) to find $\overrightarrow{FN}$.) □

In the above example, each of the vectors $\overrightarrow{AE}$, $\overrightarrow{FN}$, and $\overrightarrow{FC}$, belongs to $Span\{\boldsymbol{u},\boldsymbol{v}\}$. What about other vectors lying in the same plane as $\boldsymbol{u}$ and $\boldsymbol{v}$? Are they in the same spanning set? One may suspect, based on our experience with the above problems, that for any vector lying in this plane we can propose a procedure similar to the ones of the above example and present the vector as a linear combination of $\boldsymbol{u}$ and $\boldsymbol{v}$.

We shall prove that such a procedure exists, and therefore any two noncollinear vectors span every vector that is coplanar with them.

Theorem 1.4.3 Any vector coplanar with two noncollinear vectors is their linear combination, whose coefficients are defined uniquely.

Proof. Let $\boldsymbol{e}_1$ and $\boldsymbol{e}_2$ be two noncollinear vectors, and $\boldsymbol{a}$ be some vector coplanar with them.

If $\boldsymbol{a}$ is collinear with one of the vectors $\boldsymbol{e}_1$ or $\boldsymbol{e}_2$, the result of the theorem follows immediately from Theorem 1 of the previous subsection. If, for example, $\boldsymbol{a}$ is collinear with $\boldsymbol{e}_1$, then $\boldsymbol{a} = \alpha_1\boldsymbol{e}_1 + 0\cdot\boldsymbol{e}_2$ and α_1 is defined uniquely.

Now let us consider a *generic* (more general) situation, when $\boldsymbol{a}$ is not collinear with any of these two vectors. We will show that (i) $\boldsymbol{a}$ is a linear combination of $\boldsymbol{e}_1$ and $\boldsymbol{e}_2$, and (ii) the coefficients of this combination are defined uniquely.

(i) We can use parallel translations to bring the three vectors to a common origin, some point O. Since the three vectors are coplanar they will lie in one plane P.

Let us extend $\boldsymbol{e}_1$ and $\boldsymbol{e}_2$ into the straight lines on which they lie, and draw the lines parallel to them through the terminal point A of $\boldsymbol{a}$, as shown in Figure 9.

The points of intersection of these lines with the extensions of $\boldsymbol{e}_1$ and $\boldsymbol{e}_2$ will be labeled M and N respectively. Thus we have constructed a parallelogram $OMAN$, and according to the parallelogram rule of addition of vectors,

$$\boldsymbol{a} = \overrightarrow{OA} = \overrightarrow{OM} + \overrightarrow{ON} \quad (5)$$

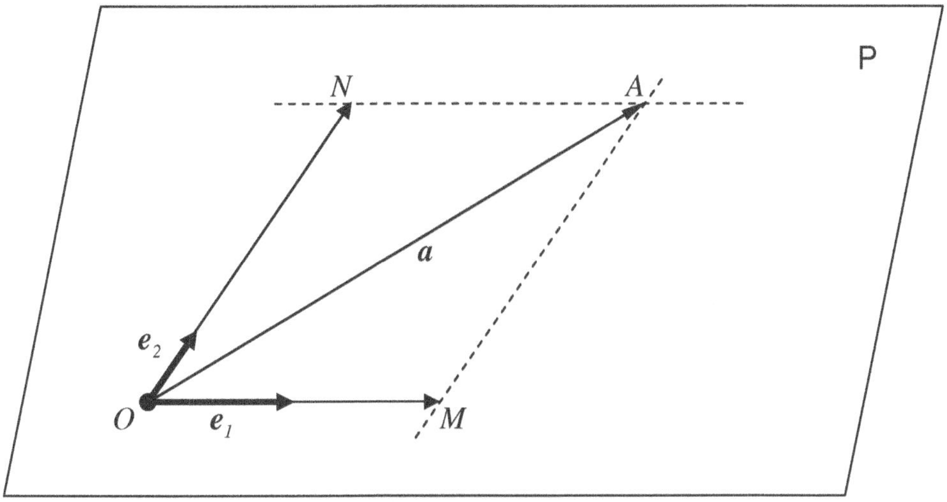

Figure 9

Since $\overrightarrow{OM}$ is collinear with $\boldsymbol{e}_1$, there exists exactly one number α_1 such that $\overrightarrow{OM} = \alpha_1\boldsymbol{e}_1$; similarly there exists exactly one such number α_2 that $\overrightarrow{ON} = \alpha_2\boldsymbol{e}_2$. After substituting these expressions for $\overrightarrow{OM}$ and $\overrightarrow{ON}$ into the last equation, we obtain

$$\boldsymbol{a} = \alpha_1\boldsymbol{e}_1 + \alpha_2\boldsymbol{e}_2, \quad (6)$$

which proves the first part of the statement of the theorem.

(ii) Now let us prove that the coefficients α_1 and α_2 of the above linear combination are defined uniquely. We can prove this both geometrically and algebraically.

Geometric proof. According to the Euclidean parallel postulate, one cannot draw more than one line parallel to a given line through a given point. Therefore, there is exactly one line that passes through A parallel to the line containing $\boldsymbol{e}_1$. Since two lines cannot intersect in more than one point (it is another axiom of Euclidean geometry), this line will cut the extension of $\boldsymbol{e}_2$ in one and only one point N. Thus, the vector $\overrightarrow{ON}$ is defined uniquely for a given $\boldsymbol{a}$, and by Theorem 1 of the previous subsection, there exists exactly one such number α_2 that $\overrightarrow{ON} = \alpha_2 \boldsymbol{e}_2$.

Similarly, M and $\overrightarrow{OM}$ are defined uniquely, and there is a unique α_1 such that $\overrightarrow{OM} = \alpha_1 \boldsymbol{e}_1$. Thus, α_1 and α_2 are unique for a given $\boldsymbol{a}$.

Algebraic proof. Suppose $\boldsymbol{a}$ is not defined uniquely as a linear combination of $\boldsymbol{e}_1$ and $\boldsymbol{e}_2$. That means that in addition to $\boldsymbol{a} = \alpha_1 \boldsymbol{e}_1 + \alpha_2 \boldsymbol{e}_2$ there exists another linear combination of these vectors that is also equal to $\boldsymbol{a}$:

$$\boldsymbol{a} = \beta_1 \boldsymbol{e}_1 + \beta_2 \boldsymbol{e}_2, \tag{7}$$

where at least one of the coefficients β_1 or β_2 is not equal to the respective α_1 or α_2; let us suppose for certainty that

$$\alpha_1 \neq \beta_1. \tag{8}$$

Since both linear combinations are equal to the same vector $\boldsymbol{a}$, we can write the equation

$$\alpha_1 \boldsymbol{e}_1 + \alpha_2 \boldsymbol{e}_2 = \beta_1 \boldsymbol{e}_1 + \beta \boldsymbol{e}_2, \tag{9}$$

which, after using properties of linear operations, can be rewritten as

$$(\alpha_1 - \beta_1)\boldsymbol{e}_1 = (\beta_2 - \alpha_2)\boldsymbol{e}_2. \tag{10}$$

Since, by our suggestion, $\alpha_1 \neq \beta_1$, we can divide both sides of this equation by a nonzero number $\alpha_1 - \beta_1$ and thus obtain:

$$\boldsymbol{e}_1 = \frac{\beta_2 - \alpha_2}{\alpha_1 - \beta_1}\boldsymbol{e}_2. \tag{11}$$

The last equation means that $\boldsymbol{e}_1$ is a scalar multiple of $\boldsymbol{e}_2$, which is impossible since these two vectors are not collinear.

Hence our suggestion that $\alpha_1 \neq \beta_1$ cannot be true, and thus $\alpha_1 = \beta_1$. Similarly, we can show that $\alpha_2 = \beta_2$. This completes the proof. □

Corollary 1 Any three coplanar vectors are linearly dependent.

Proof. Let three vectors $\boldsymbol{a}$, $\boldsymbol{b}$, and $\boldsymbol{c}$ be coplanar. Let us consider all possible situations.

(i) If two of them are noncollinear, then, according to the last theorem, the third vector is their linear combination, and by Proposition 4 of the previous subsection, these three vectors are linearly dependent.

Let us repeat the proof of this proposition for our particular case of three vectors. Suppose, $\boldsymbol{a}$ and $\boldsymbol{b}$ are noncollinear, then $\boldsymbol{c} = x\boldsymbol{a} + y\boldsymbol{b}$, and hence $\boldsymbol{c} - x\boldsymbol{a} - y\boldsymbol{b} = \boldsymbol{0}$.

Thus a linear combination of $\boldsymbol{a}$, $\boldsymbol{b}$, and $\boldsymbol{c}$ is $\boldsymbol{0}$, and at least one coefficient is not 0 (the coefficient of $\boldsymbol{c}$ is 1); therefore these three vectors are linearly dependent.

(ii) Now let us consider the situation where all three vectors are collinear. If all of these vectors are zero vectors, we can multiply them by any nonzero coefficients, and their linear combination will be $\boldsymbol{0}$, so they are linearly dependent.

If one of these vectors is nonzero, the other two are multiples of this vector. For example, if $\boldsymbol{a} \neq \boldsymbol{0}$, then $\boldsymbol{b} = k\boldsymbol{a}$, where k is some number. Then the linear combination $\boldsymbol{b} - k\boldsymbol{a} - 0 \cdot \boldsymbol{c} = \boldsymbol{0}$ has a nonzero coefficient ($\boldsymbol{b}$ is multiplied by 1), which proves the linear dependence. □

The result of Theorem 1.4.3 enables us to call any two noncollinear vectors in a plane a *basis* in this plane. Let us also notice that two noncollinear vectors are linearly independent, as we have established in Proposition 1 of the previous section. It is important since, as we have already noticed, the requirement of linear independence will be included in the general definition of a basis.

We always assume that the vectors of a basis are arranged in a certain order, for instance $\boldsymbol{e}_1$ is the first, and $\boldsymbol{e}_2$ - the second vector of the basis. Thus the vectors of a basis in a plane form an *ordered pair* of vectors.

Definition. A *basis in a plane of vectors* is any ordered pair $\boldsymbol{e}_1$, $\boldsymbol{e}_2$ of noncollinear vectors from this plane. If $\boldsymbol{a} = \alpha_1\boldsymbol{e}_1 + \alpha_2\boldsymbol{e}_2$, this linear combination is called the *expansion of* $\boldsymbol{a}$ *in the basis* $\{\boldsymbol{e}_1, \boldsymbol{e}_2\}$, and α_1, α_2 are called the *coordinates* (or *components*) of $\boldsymbol{a}$ in the basis $\{\boldsymbol{e}_1, \boldsymbol{e}_2\}$.

When proving the last part of the latter theorem, we have proved that two vectors with different components cannot be equal: $\alpha_1\boldsymbol{e}_1 + \alpha_2\boldsymbol{e}_2 = \beta_1\boldsymbol{e}_1 + \beta\boldsymbol{e}_2$ only if $\alpha_1 = \beta_1$ and $\alpha_2 = \beta_2$. It is obvious that two linear combinations of the same vectors ($\boldsymbol{e}_1$ and $\boldsymbol{e}_2$) with the same coefficients are equal, and hence we have the following result:

Theorem 1.4.4 Two vectors are equal if and only if their coordinates (components) in a given basis are equal.

Corollary 1 As soon as a basis in a plane is chosen, every vector of the plane is assigned *exactly one* ordered pair of numbers.

Proof. First let us explain the phrase *exactly one*. It means: *one and not more than one*. Thus two things are asserted: (1) every vector is assigned an ordered pair of numbers and (2) a vector cannot be assigned two (or more) different ordered pairs. The expression *exactly one* is often used to claim that an object exists and at the same time such an object is unique. One can express the same by saying *one and only one*.

Now let us prove the statement of the corollary.

We have proved in Theorem 1.4.3 that such a pair exists for every vector: this is a pair of its coordinates (components) in the given basis. Also, it follows from Theorem

1.4.4 that a different pair of coordinates cannot belong to the same vector: vectors are equal only if their components are respectively equal); hence one vector cannot be assigned two (or more) distinct ordered pairs of numbers. □

We can also show that whenever an ordered pair of numbers is given, we can find such a vector in a plane that this vector will have the numbers of the ordered pair as its components in a given basis. Moreover, for a given pair of numbers and a given basis there will be exactly one such vector.

In order to prove the existence of such a vector we just have to repeat the construction of Theorem 1.4.3 in reverse: given a pair of numbers (α_1, α_2) and a basis $\boldsymbol{e}_1$, $\boldsymbol{e}_2$, bring the origins of the vectors to some point O and construct vectors $\overrightarrow{OM} = \alpha_1 \boldsymbol{e}_1$ and $\overrightarrow{ON} = \alpha_2 \boldsymbol{e}_2$. The sum $\overrightarrow{OM} + \overrightarrow{ON} = \alpha_1 \boldsymbol{e}_1 + \alpha_2 \boldsymbol{e}_2$ will be a vector with the components (α_1, α_2) in the basis $\{\boldsymbol{e}_1, \boldsymbol{e}_2\}$. This vector is unique according to Theorem 1.4.4: any other vector will have components different from (α_1, α_2).

Thus we have established the following correspondence between the vectors of a plane and the set of ordered pairs of numbers: as soon as a basis in a plane of vectors is chosen, *there is exactly one ordered pair of numbers for every vector and exactly one vector of the plane for every ordered pair of numbers.*

Such a correspondence is called a *one-one correspondence* (or a *bijection*) between the members of two sets (in our case, the set of all vectors of a plane and the set of all ordered pairs of numbers).

The existence of such a correspondence is quite a remarkable result, since it will allow us to use algebra to describe vectors, which are geometric objects. Let us summarize what we have learned in the following theorem:

Theorem 1.4.5 Given a plane of vectors, there is a *one-one* correspondence between the vectors of the plane and the ordered pairs of real numbers that represent their coordinates in a given basis:

$$\boldsymbol{a} = \alpha_1 \boldsymbol{e}_1 + \alpha_2 \boldsymbol{e}_2 \quad \leftrightarrow \quad (\alpha_1, \alpha_2). \tag{12}$$

Usually it is more convenient to write an ordered pair of numbers in a so-called column form, or as a *two-column*; then the above correspondence can be written as

$$\boldsymbol{a} = \alpha_1 \boldsymbol{e}_1 + \alpha_2 \boldsymbol{e}_2 \quad \leftrightarrow \quad \begin{bmatrix} \alpha_1 \\ \alpha_2 \end{bmatrix}. \tag{13}$$

It follows from the properties of linear operations with vectors that this correspondence is preserved by linear operations, i.e. the following two statements hold:

Theorem 1.4.6 If two vectors are added, their respective coordinates are also added:

$$\text{if } \boldsymbol{a} \leftrightarrow \begin{bmatrix} \alpha_1 \\ \alpha_2 \end{bmatrix} \text{ and } \boldsymbol{b} \leftrightarrow \begin{bmatrix} \beta_1 \\ \beta_2 \end{bmatrix}, \quad \text{then} \quad \boldsymbol{a}+\boldsymbol{b} \leftrightarrow \begin{bmatrix} \alpha_1+\beta_1 \\ \alpha_2+\beta_2 \end{bmatrix} . \tag{14}$$

Theorem 1.4.7 If a vector is multiplied by a number, its coordinates are multiplied by this number:

$$\text{if } \boldsymbol{a} \leftrightarrow \begin{bmatrix} \alpha_1 \\ \alpha_2 \end{bmatrix}, \quad \text{then } k\boldsymbol{a} \leftrightarrow \begin{bmatrix} k\alpha_1 \\ k\alpha_2 \end{bmatrix} . \tag{15}$$

One can also show that these two statements together are equivalent to a single statement concerning linear operations with vectors and their coordinates:

Theorem 1.4.8 If a vector is a linear combination of two vectors, its coordinates are the respective linear combinations of the coordinates of these two vectors:

$$\text{if } \boldsymbol{a} \leftrightarrow \begin{bmatrix} \alpha_1 \\ \alpha_2 \end{bmatrix} \text{ and } \boldsymbol{b} \leftrightarrow \begin{bmatrix} \beta_1 \\ \beta_2 \end{bmatrix}, \text{ then } x\boldsymbol{a}+y\boldsymbol{b} \leftrightarrow \begin{bmatrix} x\alpha_1+y\beta_1 \\ x\alpha_2+y\beta_2 \end{bmatrix}, \tag{16}$$

where x and y are some numbers.

Proof. We just use the properties of linear operations:

$$x\boldsymbol{a}+y\boldsymbol{b} = x(\alpha_1\boldsymbol{e}_1+\alpha_2\boldsymbol{e}_2)+y(\beta_1\boldsymbol{e}_1+\beta_2\boldsymbol{e}_2) = (x\alpha_1+y\beta_1)\boldsymbol{e}_1+(x\alpha_2+y\beta_2)\boldsymbol{e}_2 \leftrightarrow \begin{bmatrix} x\alpha_1+y\beta_1 \\ x\alpha_2+y\beta_2 \end{bmatrix}$$

Now let us define the operations of addition and scalar multiplication (multiplication by numbers) in the set of all ordered pairs of numbers, or the set of all 2-columns. This set will be denoted R^2.

Definition. For any columns $\begin{bmatrix} \alpha_1 \\ \alpha_2 \end{bmatrix}$ and $\begin{bmatrix} \beta_1 \\ \beta_2 \end{bmatrix}$ and any number x,

$$\begin{bmatrix} \alpha_1 \\ \alpha_2 \end{bmatrix} + \begin{bmatrix} \beta_1 \\ \beta_2 \end{bmatrix} = \begin{bmatrix} \alpha_1+\beta_1 \\ \alpha_2+\beta_2 \end{bmatrix}; \quad x\begin{bmatrix} \alpha_1 \\ \alpha_2 \end{bmatrix} = \begin{bmatrix} x\alpha_1 \\ x\alpha_2 \end{bmatrix}. \tag{17}$$

It is easy to show that the above definitions given by two formulae, is equivalent to the following rule for constructing linear combinations of two columns:

$$x\begin{bmatrix} \alpha_1 \\ \alpha_2 \end{bmatrix} + y\begin{bmatrix} \beta_1 \\ \beta_2 \end{bmatrix} = \begin{bmatrix} x\alpha_1+y\beta_1 \\ x\alpha_2+y\beta_2 \end{bmatrix}, \tag{18}$$

where x and y are some numbers (the coefficients of the linear combination).

Also, one can verify that these operations in R^2 possess exactly the same properties (1-8) as the properties of linear operations with vectors, established in Section 1.2. Because of this we can call R^2 a *linear vector space*. In general, a *linear vector space* is a set of objects (of any nature) with operations on them that possess the properties (1-8). (For brevity we will often replace the long phrase *linear vector space* with a shorter expression *vector space* or just *space*).

Thus we have established a remarkable correspondence between vector spaces of different types: a plane of geometric vectors and the set R^2 of all ordered pairs of real numbers (or 2-columns):

(i) When a basis in a plane is chosen, each vector is assigned an ordered pair of numbers (or a 2-column), which are the coordinates of the vector in this basis, and this correspondence between the vectors and pairs of numbers (2-columns) is one-to-one.

(ii) Also, this correspondence is preserved by the linear operations defined in the two spaces: the sum of two vectors corresponds to the sum of their corresponding columns, and the scalar multiple of a vector corresponds to the scalar multiple of the corresponding column with the same coefficient. (One can also say that a linear combination of vectors corresponds to the linear combination of the corresponding columns with the same respective coefficients).

Any such correspondence between two vector spaces that have the above properties, namely *(i) it is one- one*, and *(ii) it is preserved by the linear operations*, is called an *isomorphism* between the two vector spaces. Also, we say that one space is *isomorphic* to the other.

The word *isomorphic* means "having the same shape". It is always applied to sets of objects that are identical from a certain viewpoint. In our case, a plane of vectors and the space R^2 are not different from the point of view of linear algebra.

Another example of an isomorphism has been established earlier in the course: a correspondence between a line of vectors (a set of all vectors collinear to each other) and the set of all real numbers R.

Since from the viewpoint of linear algebra a plane of vectors is identical to R^2, we shall for the sake of convenience identify vectors using the corresponding pairs of numbers or columns.

For example, we shall write $\boldsymbol{a} = \begin{bmatrix} 5 \\ 9 \end{bmatrix}$ and say "vector $\boldsymbol{a}$ is equal to $\begin{bmatrix} 5 \\ 9 \end{bmatrix}$" instead of writing $\boldsymbol{a} = 5\boldsymbol{e}_1 + 9\boldsymbol{e}_2 \quad \leftrightarrow \quad \begin{bmatrix} 5 \\ 9 \end{bmatrix}$ and saying that "the coordinates of vector $\boldsymbol{a}$ in the given basis are 5 and 9 and thus it corresponds to the column $\begin{bmatrix} 5 \\ 9 \end{bmatrix}$ from R^2".

In general, if $\{\boldsymbol{e}_1, \boldsymbol{e}_2\}$ is a basis in a plane and $\boldsymbol{a} = \alpha_1\boldsymbol{e}_1 + \alpha_2\boldsymbol{e}_2$, we shall write $\boldsymbol{a} = \begin{bmatrix} \alpha_1 \\ \alpha_2 \end{bmatrix}$. Since for the basis vectors we have $\boldsymbol{e}_1 = 1 \cdot \boldsymbol{e}_1 + 0 \cdot \boldsymbol{e}_2$ and $\boldsymbol{e}_2 = 0 \cdot \boldsymbol{e}_1 + 1 \cdot \boldsymbol{e}_2$, we shall write for them

$$\boldsymbol{e}_1 = \begin{bmatrix} 1 \\ 0 \end{bmatrix}; \quad \boldsymbol{e}_2 = \begin{bmatrix} 0 \\ 1 \end{bmatrix}. \tag{19}$$

The basis $\left\{\begin{bmatrix}1\\0\end{bmatrix},\begin{bmatrix}0\\1\end{bmatrix}\right\}$ is called the *standard basis* in R^2. Let us notice that it can be identified with any basis in a plane of vectors; yet after a basis in a plane has been chosen, the coordinates of all the vectors in the plane are fixed.

Example 3. In Figure 10 below, a few coplanar vectors, namely $\boldsymbol{e_1},\boldsymbol{e_2},\boldsymbol{i},\boldsymbol{j},\boldsymbol{a},\boldsymbol{b}$ are shown. To facilitate calculations, the plane is covered by a square grid.

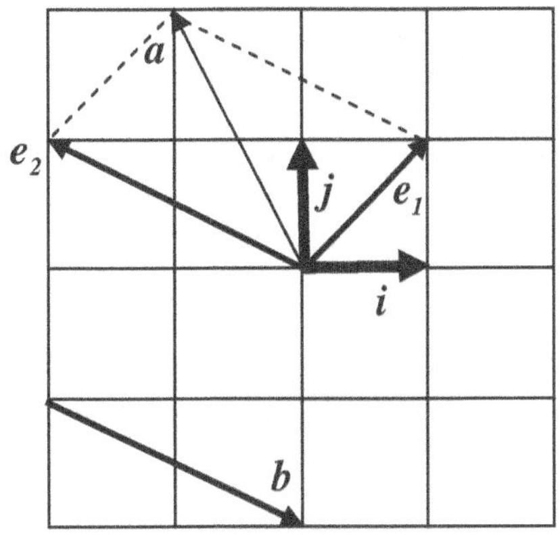

Figure 10

Also for convenience some of these vectors are drawn emanating from the same point. This way it is easy to see, for example, that

$$\boldsymbol{a} = \boldsymbol{e_1} + \boldsymbol{e_2}; \quad (20)$$

$$\text{also} \quad \boldsymbol{a} = -\boldsymbol{i} + 2\boldsymbol{j}. \quad (21)$$

Each of the pairs $\{\boldsymbol{e}_1,\boldsymbol{e}_2\}$ and $\{\boldsymbol{i},\boldsymbol{j}\}$ consists of two noncollinear vectors and therefore each of these pairs is a basis in the plane containing these vectors. Let us find the 2-columns corresponding to the vector $\boldsymbol{a}$ shown in the diagram in the following two cases:

(i) $\{\boldsymbol{e}_1,\boldsymbol{e}_2\}$ corresponds to the standard basis in R^2, i.e. $\boldsymbol{e_1} = \begin{bmatrix}1\\0\end{bmatrix}$; $\boldsymbol{e}_2 = \begin{bmatrix}0\\1\end{bmatrix}$.

(ii) $\{\boldsymbol{i},\boldsymbol{j}\}$ corresponds to the standard basis in R^2, i.e. $\boldsymbol{i} = \begin{bmatrix}1\\0\end{bmatrix}$; $\boldsymbol{j} = \begin{bmatrix}0\\1\end{bmatrix}$.

We shall see that the same vector $\boldsymbol{a}$ is represented by a different column in each of these cases.

(i) If we assume that $\{\boldsymbol{e}_1,\boldsymbol{e}_2\}$ is the basis corresponding to the standard one in R^2,

then $\boldsymbol{e_1} = \begin{bmatrix}1\\0\end{bmatrix}$; $\boldsymbol{e_2} = \begin{bmatrix}0\\1\end{bmatrix}$, and $\boldsymbol{a} = \boldsymbol{e_1} + \boldsymbol{e_2} = \begin{bmatrix}1\\0\end{bmatrix} + \begin{bmatrix}0\\1\end{bmatrix} = \begin{bmatrix}1\\1\end{bmatrix}$.

The coordinates of $\boldsymbol{a}$ in the basis $\{\boldsymbol{i},\boldsymbol{j}\}$ are (-1) and 2; still we cannot identify $\boldsymbol{a}$ with the column $\begin{bmatrix}-1\\2\end{bmatrix}$, since the basis $\{\boldsymbol{i},\boldsymbol{j}\}$ is not identified with the standard basis. Sometimes a fancier notation is used in order to present a vector in a column form:

$$\boldsymbol{a}=\begin{bmatrix}-1\\2\end{bmatrix}_{\{i,j\}}, \tag{22}$$

where the subscript after the column reminds us that the basis $\{\boldsymbol{i},\boldsymbol{j}\}$ is not in correspondence with the standard basis of R^2, and what we really mean is that the coordinates of $\boldsymbol{a}$ in the basis $\{\boldsymbol{i},\boldsymbol{j}\}$ are -1 and 2: $\boldsymbol{a}=-\boldsymbol{i}+2\boldsymbol{j}$.

We can use the last expression to verify that $\boldsymbol{a}=\begin{bmatrix}1\\1\end{bmatrix}$ in the standard basis. In order to do this, we have to substitute into the equation $\boldsymbol{a}=-\boldsymbol{i}+2\boldsymbol{j}$ the expressions for $\boldsymbol{i}$ and $\boldsymbol{j}$ in the standard basis. These are not very easy to find directly from the diagram in Figure 10. We can however do the following: express $\boldsymbol{e}_1$ and $\boldsymbol{e}_2$ in terms of $\boldsymbol{i}$ and $\boldsymbol{j}$ from the diagram, and then from these expressions determine $\boldsymbol{i}$ and $\boldsymbol{j}$ in terms of $\boldsymbol{e}_1$ and $\boldsymbol{e}_2$.

It is obvious from the diagram that

$$\begin{cases}\boldsymbol{e}_1= \ \ \boldsymbol{i}+\boldsymbol{j}\\ \boldsymbol{e}_2=-2\boldsymbol{i}+\boldsymbol{j}\end{cases}. \tag{23}$$

By subtracting the second equation from the first one, we obtain

$$\boldsymbol{e}_1-\boldsymbol{e}_2=3\boldsymbol{i}, \tag{24}$$

whence we can find $\boldsymbol{i}=\frac{1}{3}(\boldsymbol{e}_1-\boldsymbol{e}_2)$. Then the first equation of the above system (23) can be rewritten as $\boldsymbol{e}_1=\frac{1}{3}(\boldsymbol{e}_1-\boldsymbol{e}_2)+\boldsymbol{j}$, and therefore, $\boldsymbol{j}=\frac{2}{3}\boldsymbol{e}_1+\frac{1}{3}\boldsymbol{e}_2$. Now we can obtain the columns representing $\boldsymbol{i}$ and $\boldsymbol{j}$:

$$\begin{cases}\boldsymbol{i}=\frac{1}{3}\boldsymbol{e}_1-\frac{1}{3}\boldsymbol{e}_2=\frac{1}{3}\begin{bmatrix}1\\0\end{bmatrix}-\frac{1}{3}\begin{bmatrix}0\\1\end{bmatrix}=\begin{bmatrix}\frac{1}{3}\\-\frac{1}{3}\end{bmatrix}\\ \boldsymbol{j}=\frac{2}{3}\boldsymbol{e}_1+\frac{1}{3}\boldsymbol{e}_2=\frac{2}{3}\begin{bmatrix}1\\0\end{bmatrix}+\frac{1}{3}\begin{bmatrix}0\\1\end{bmatrix}=\begin{bmatrix}\frac{2}{3}\\\frac{1}{3}\end{bmatrix}\end{cases}. \tag{25}$$

We can substitute these into the expansion of $\boldsymbol{a}$ in the basis $\{\boldsymbol{i},\boldsymbol{j}\}$ to obtain the column representing $\boldsymbol{a}$:

$$\boldsymbol{a}=-\boldsymbol{i}+2\boldsymbol{j}=-\begin{bmatrix}\frac{1}{3}\\-\frac{1}{3}\end{bmatrix}+2\begin{bmatrix}\frac{2}{3}\\\frac{1}{3}\end{bmatrix}=\begin{bmatrix}-\frac{1}{3}+2\cdot\frac{2}{3}\\\frac{1}{3}+2\cdot\frac{1}{3}\end{bmatrix}=\begin{bmatrix}1\\1\end{bmatrix}. \tag{26}$$

(ii) Now let us assume that $\{\boldsymbol{i},\boldsymbol{j}\}$ corresponds to the standard basis in R^2, which means that $\boldsymbol{i}=\begin{bmatrix}1\\0\end{bmatrix}$; $\boldsymbol{j}=\begin{bmatrix}0\\1\end{bmatrix}$, and $\boldsymbol{a}=-\boldsymbol{i}+2\boldsymbol{j}=(-1)\begin{bmatrix}1\\0\end{bmatrix}+2\begin{bmatrix}0\\1\end{bmatrix}=\begin{bmatrix}-1\\2\end{bmatrix}$.

(It should be noticed that the choice of $\{i,j\}$ as the basis corresponding to the standard one in R^2 is the most common choice; hereafter we shall suggest this choice unless specified otherwise).

Since in this case $\{e_1,e_2\}$ is not identified with the standard basis anymore, we rewrite the expansion $a = e_1 + e_2$ in column form as $a = \begin{bmatrix} 1 \\ 1 \end{bmatrix}_{\{e_1,e_2\}}$. One can use the expansions (23) for e_1 and e_2 to show that this column is transformed into $\begin{bmatrix} -1 \\ 2 \end{bmatrix}$ in the standard basis.

Now let us subject vector b from the diagram to a similar consideration. Although this vector does not emanate from the common origin of other vectors, it can be carried there by means of a parallel translation, and one can find the expansions for b in these two bases:

in the basis $\{e_1,e_2\}$: $b = -e_2 = 0 \cdot e_1 + (-1)e_2 = \begin{bmatrix} 0 \\ -1 \end{bmatrix}_{\{e_1,e_2\}}$, and

in the basis $\{i,j\}$: $b = 2i - j = \begin{bmatrix} 2 \\ -1 \end{bmatrix}_{\{i,j\}}$.

(i) If $\{e_1,e_2\}$ corresponds to the standard basis of R^2, we can substitute the columns representing i and j from equations (23) in the last expansion and obtain the column $\begin{bmatrix} 0 \\ -1 \end{bmatrix}$, representing b in the standard basis (verify this).

(ii) If $\{i,j\}$ is identified with the standard basis in R^2, we can substitute $e_2 = -2i + j$ into the expansion $b = -e_2$ to obtain $b = 2i - j = \begin{bmatrix} 2 \\ -1 \end{bmatrix}$, and the latter column represents b in the standard basis. ▫

Let us emphasize that when writing a vector as a column, we always suggest that a certain basis $\{e_1,e_2\}$ correspond to the standard basis in R^2; in some other basis $\{b_1,b_2\}$ the same vector a will have different components and will be therefore presented by a different column.

If, for instance, $a = \alpha_1 e_1 + \alpha_2 e_2 = \beta_1 e_1 + \beta_2 e_2$ and $\{e_1,e_2\}$ is the basis corresponding to the standard basis in R^2, then

$$e_1 = \begin{bmatrix} 1 \\ 0 \end{bmatrix}, \quad e_2 = \begin{bmatrix} 0 \\ 1 \end{bmatrix}, \quad \text{and } a = \begin{bmatrix} \alpha_1 \\ \alpha_2 \end{bmatrix} = \begin{bmatrix} \beta_1 \\ \beta_2 \end{bmatrix}_{\{b_1,b_2\}}. \tag{27}$$

Here we have adopted the notation of the last example: for any basis other than the standard one, we shall write a label for the basis as a subscript following a column of coordinates.

For the sake of brevity we shall often say that a basis in a plane is standard instead of saying that it corresponds to the standard basis in R^2. For example, we shall say "$\{e_1,e_2\}$ is the standard basis" instead of saying "$\{e_1,e_2\}$ corresponds to the standard basis in R^2". Also, we shall often identify a plane of vectors with R^2.

As we have already mentioned, $\{i,j\}$ will be identified with the standard basis in R^2 if not specifies otherwise. This basis ($\{i,j\}$) has a special geometric meaning that makes it more convenient for solving problems in analytic geometry; we shall discuss that meaning and define such a basis later in the course.

We have already shown in the beginning of this subsection how a coordinate axis can be associated with a nonzero vector. If a basis $\{e_1,e_2\}$ is given in a plane, we can translate the vectors of the basis so that they will emanate from the same point *O*. Then we can associate a coordinate axis originating at *O* with each of the vectors of the basis. Thus we have introduced on the plane a so-called *Cartesian coordinate system*. Point *O* is called the *origin* of the coordinate system, and the axes associated with e_1 and e_2 are called respectively the first and the second coordinate axes or the axes of *abscissas (Ox)* and *ordinates (Oy)*.

Now every point *A* of the plane can be connect to the origin *O* by means of a vector $\overrightarrow{OA}$ emanating from the origin *O* and ending at that point *A*. Such a vector $\overrightarrow{OA}$ will be called the *position vector* of point *A*, since it completely determines the location (position) of the point with respect to the origin. The components (coordinates) of the position vector $\overrightarrow{OA}$ in the given basis are also called the *affine coordinates* of point *A*. The word *affine*, which is often omitted for brevity, means that we consider a plane as a set of points; such a plane is called an *affine* plane. We shall often omit this scary word, since it will be always clear whether we mean a plane of points (affine plane) or a plane of vectors.

In Figure 11, point *A* has the coordinates (x_A, y_A), which are also the coordinates (components) of its position vector $\overrightarrow{OA}$. Similarly the coordinates of point B, the endpoint of its position vector $\overrightarrow{OB}$, are (x_B, y_B).

Since a basis vector determines the positive direction on the respective coordinate axis, both coordinates of *A* and the abscissa of *B* are positive, whereas the ordinate of *B* is negative: $y_B < 0$.

If a point lies on a coordinate axis, one of its coordinates will be 0; for instance in Figure 11, $x_M = 0$. Needless to say that the coordinates of the terminal points of the basis vectors e_1 and e_2 are (1,0) and (0,1) respectively.

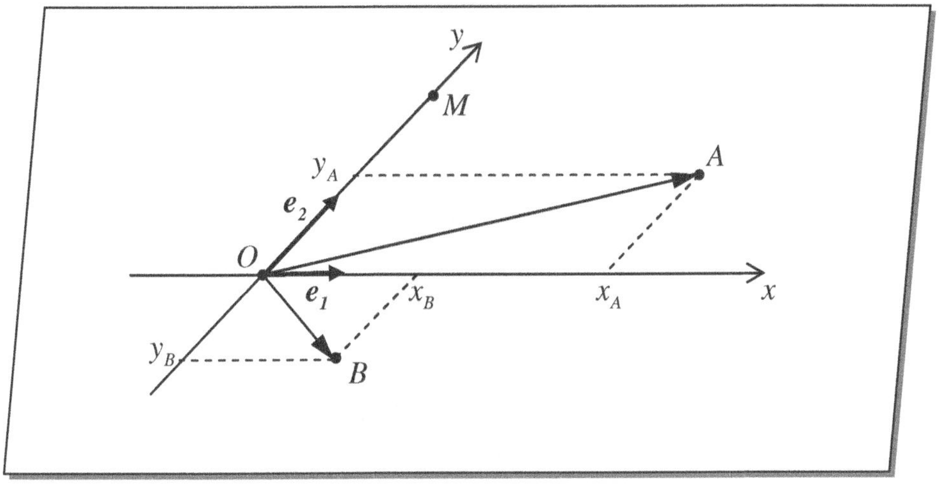

Figure 11

It is easy to show that as in the case of a single coordinate axis (Theorem 1.4.2), the coordinates of any vector lying in a Cartesian plane can be determined as the differences between the affine coordinates of its terminal point and the origin:

Theorem 1.4.9 If A and B are two points in a Cartesian plane, and their respective coordinates are (x_A, y_A) and (x_B, y_B), then the coordinates of the vector $\overrightarrow{AB}$ connecting these points are $(x_B - x_A, y_B - y_A)$.

Proof. By definition of addition of vectors, $\overrightarrow{OA} + \overrightarrow{AB} = \overrightarrow{OB}$ (see Figure 12), hence $\overrightarrow{AB} = \overrightarrow{OB} - \overrightarrow{OA} = (x_B\boldsymbol{e}_1 + y_B\boldsymbol{e}_2) - (x_A\boldsymbol{e}_1 + y_A\boldsymbol{e}_2) = (x_B - x_A)\boldsymbol{e}_1 + (y_B - y_A)\boldsymbol{e}_2$, which proves the statement of the theorem. □

Let us notice that if vector $\boldsymbol{v} = \overrightarrow{AB}$ is translated so that its origin coincides with O, it will become a position vector of some point C, with the affine coordinates

$$\begin{cases} x_C = x_B - x_A \\ y_C = y_B - y_A \end{cases}. \tag{28}$$

Thus, *every point of a Cartesian plane is assigned exactly one vector* lying in the plane, namely – its position vector. Let us notice that all the vectors equal to each other are viewed as a single vector. For example, for the plane shown in Figure 12, only vector $\overrightarrow{OC} = \boldsymbol{v}$ is assigned to point C; all the other vectors that are equal to $\boldsymbol{v}$, e.g. $\overrightarrow{AB}, \overrightarrow{MN}$, and infinitely many others, are identified with $\overrightarrow{OC} = \boldsymbol{v}$.

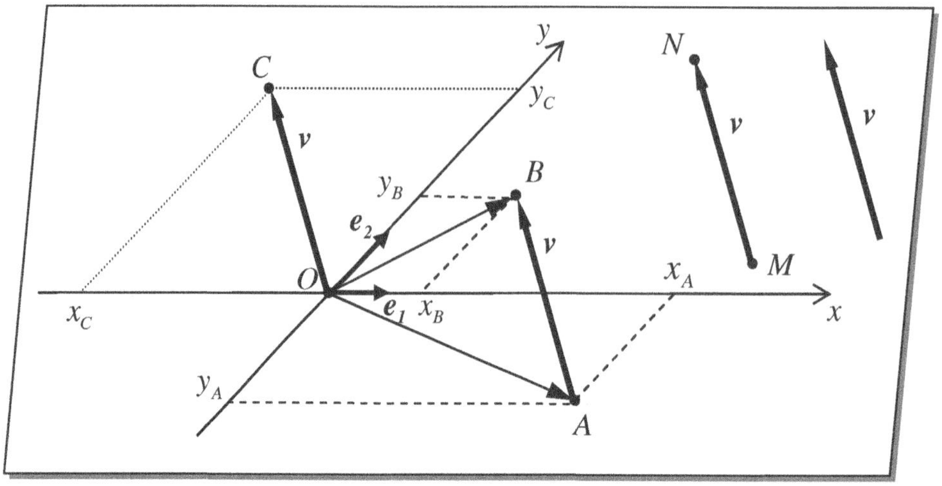

Figure 12

The converse is also true: *given a vector from a plane* (for example, ***v*** in the above diagram), we can translate its origin to the origin of a Cartesian coordinate system in order to make it a position vector; then *it will determine exactly one point* (point *C* in this example) of the plane.

Therefore we have established a *one-one correspondence* between a plane as a set of points (called an *affine plane*) and the *associated* plane of all the position vectors of these points.

Since a plane of vectors is isomorphic to R^2, we can view R^2 as the space *associated* with an affine plane. In other words, we can identify the affine coordinates of a point with a column that represents its position vector in R^2. This provides us with powerful algebraic tools for solving geometrical problems. These tools constitute the subject of *analytic geometry* (geometry by formulae).

We shall utilize some notations that should be explained. To present points in a Cartesian plane we shall write things like $A(\alpha_1,\alpha_2)$, or $A=(\alpha_1,\alpha_2)$, or $A=\begin{bmatrix}\alpha_1\\ \alpha_2\end{bmatrix}$

Each of these formulae means that we assume a coordinate system based on some basis $\{\boldsymbol{e}_1,\boldsymbol{e}_2\}$, in which the position vector of point *A* is

$$\overrightarrow{OA}=\alpha_1\boldsymbol{e}_1+\alpha_2\boldsymbol{e}_2=\begin{bmatrix}\alpha_1\\ \alpha_2\end{bmatrix}. \qquad (29)$$

It is also suggested that the basis $\{\boldsymbol{e}_1,\boldsymbol{e}_2\}$ corresponds to the standard basis in R^2.

For example, the short phrase "points *A*(2, -1) and *B*(3,5) are given" means the following:

Points A and B lie in some plane, where a Cartesian coordinate system is introduced. The basis $\{e_1, e_2\}$ of this coordinate system corresponds to the standard basis in R^2, and the position vectors of these points A and B in this basis are respectively

$$\overrightarrow{OA} = 2e_1 - e_2 = \begin{bmatrix} 2 \\ -1 \end{bmatrix} \text{ and } \overrightarrow{OB} = 3e_1 + 5e_2 = \begin{bmatrix} 3 \\ 5 \end{bmatrix}.$$

Even though we present points by pairs of numbers or 2-columns, we should not forget that operations (e.g., addition and multiplication by numbers) are defined for vectors only, not for the points!

Let us consider an interesting application of vectors in Cartesian coordinate systems, - a problem of finding a point that divides a given segment in a given ratio.

Example 4. Points $A(-2, 1)$ and $B(8, 7)$ are given. Find the coordinates of a point that divides AB in the ratio 2:3 counting from A.

Solution. We are going to find the coordinates of such a point M that
$AM : MB = 2:3$.

Let us draw a diagram that will help us to visualize the situation (Figure 13). We suggest that the origin of the coordinate system is located at some point O, shown in the diagram. Now let us find the coordinates of $\overrightarrow{OM}$, the position vector of point M: the coordinates of this vector will be the coordinates of M.

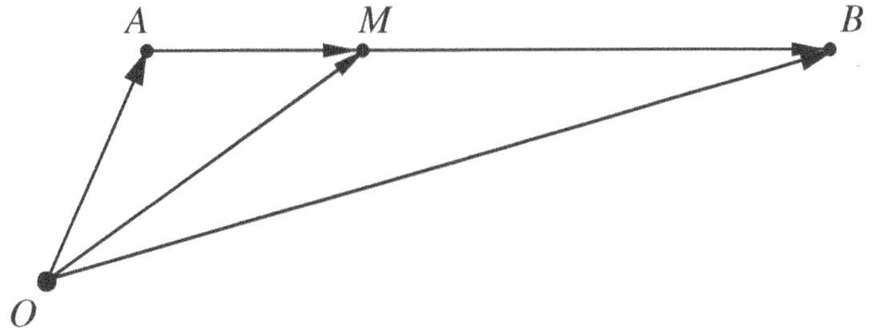

Figure 13

Since $AM : MB = 2:3$, it is easy to find that $\overrightarrow{AM} = \frac{2}{5}\overrightarrow{AB}$.

(Really, since point M lies on AB, the vectors $\overrightarrow{AM}, \overrightarrow{MB}$, and $\overrightarrow{AB}$ are parallel, and $AM : MB = 2:3$ leads to $\overrightarrow{MB} = \frac{3}{2}\overrightarrow{AM}$. Then from $\overrightarrow{AM} + \overrightarrow{MB} = \overrightarrow{AB}$ we obtain:
$\overrightarrow{AM} + \frac{3}{2}\overrightarrow{AM} = \overrightarrow{AB}; \ \Rightarrow \frac{5}{2}\overrightarrow{AM} = \overrightarrow{AB}; \ \Rightarrow \overrightarrow{AM} = \frac{2}{5}\overrightarrow{AB}$.)

Now we can find the desired vector $\overrightarrow{OM}$:

$$\overrightarrow{OM} = \overrightarrow{OA} + \overrightarrow{AM} = \overrightarrow{OA} + \frac{2}{5}\overrightarrow{AB} = \overrightarrow{OA} + \frac{2}{5}\left(\overrightarrow{OB} - \overrightarrow{OA}\right) = \frac{3}{5}\overrightarrow{OA} + \frac{2}{5}\overrightarrow{OB} =$$
$$= \frac{3}{5}\begin{bmatrix} -2 \\ 1 \end{bmatrix} + \frac{2}{5}\begin{bmatrix} 8 \\ 7 \end{bmatrix} = \begin{bmatrix} -\frac{6}{5} + \frac{16}{5} \\ \frac{3}{5} + \frac{14}{5} \end{bmatrix} = \begin{bmatrix} 2 \\ \frac{17}{5} \end{bmatrix}. \qquad (30)$$

Thus, the coordinates of M are $(2, \frac{17}{5})$. □

Remark 1. Let us notice that the method applied in this problem can be used for finding the point that divides a given segment in any given ratio and thus for obtaining a general formula for the coordinates of such a point.

Remark 2. The method is also universal in some other sense: it fits for any Cartesian plane, no matter what is the basis of the coordinate system. Our result does not depend on such geometric particularities as, for instance, the lengths of the vectors constituting the basis or an angle between them: since we are dealing with the coordinates, our solution is algebraic.

(iii) The space of geometric vectors and R^3.

First of all we will be interested to know, how many vectors constitute a basis in space, and whether these vectors must satisfy some conditions. All the bases we have dealt with in the past consisted of sets of vectors that were linearly independent and spanned the whole set of vectors under consideration (a line or a plane of vectors).

Therefore we shall start with proving the necessary and sufficient condition for linear independence in space, and then determine how many vectors span the space.

Theorem 1.4.10 Three vectors are linearly dependent if and only if they are coplanar.

Proof. We have already proved in Corollary 1 of Theorem1.4.3 that any three coplanar vectors are linearly dependent. Now let us prove that three linearly dependent vectors are necessarily coplanar.

Suppose three vectors, $\boldsymbol{a}$, $\boldsymbol{b}$, and $\boldsymbol{c}$, are linearly dependent; then according to Proposition 4, one of them is a linear combination of the other two, for example $\boldsymbol{a}$ is a linear combination of $\boldsymbol{b}$ and $\boldsymbol{c}$: $\boldsymbol{a} = x\boldsymbol{b} + y\boldsymbol{c}$, where x and y are some numbers. Let us prove that $\boldsymbol{a}$ is coplanar with $\boldsymbol{b}$ and $\boldsymbol{c}$.

Since a scalar multiple of a vector is collinear with the vector, vectors $x\boldsymbol{b}$ and $y\boldsymbol{c}$ lie in the same plane as $\boldsymbol{b}$ and $\boldsymbol{c}$.

According to the definition (triangle rule) of addition, the sum of two vectors always lie in the same plane as the vectors constituting the sum: it follows from the axioms of Euclidean geometry that any three points (for example, A, B, and C in the first diagram of Figure 14) lie in one plane, and a straight segment with its endpoints in a plane (segment CB in our case) lies completely in this plane.

Therefore, vector $\boldsymbol{a} = \overrightarrow{CB} = \overrightarrow{CA} + \overrightarrow{AB} = x\boldsymbol{b} + y\boldsymbol{c}$ lies in the same plane as $x\boldsymbol{b}$ and $y\boldsymbol{c}$ and hence in the same plane as $\boldsymbol{b}$ and $\boldsymbol{c}$. □

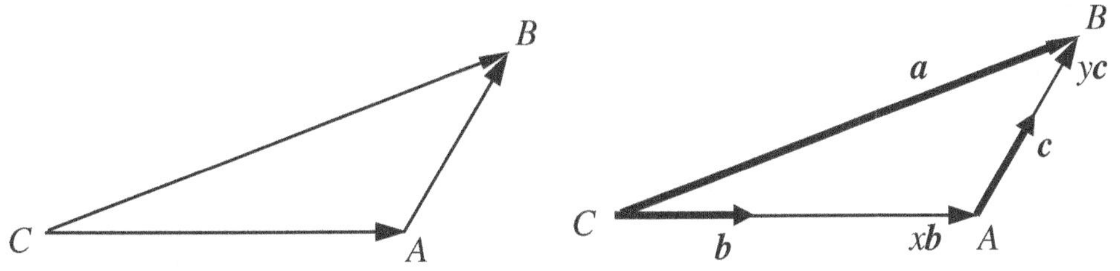

Figure 14

<u>Corollary 1.</u> Three noncoplanar vectors are linearly independent.

<u>Proof.</u> It is easy to prove the statement by contradiction. Let us suppose that there exist three vectors that are linearly dependent but not coplanar. This would contradict the above theorem, which claims that three linearly dependent vectors are always coplanar. Therefore, three coplanar vectors cannot be linearly dependent. □

Now let us prove that three noncoplanar vectors span the whole space of geometric vectors.

<u>Theorem 1.4.11</u> Every vector is a uniquely defined linear combination of three noncoplanar vectors.

Proof. Let $\{\boldsymbol{e}_1, \boldsymbol{e}_2, \boldsymbol{e}_3\}$ be three noncoplanar vectors. We have to prove two statements:

(i) Every vector is a linear combination of $\boldsymbol{e}_1, \boldsymbol{e}_2$, and $\boldsymbol{e}_3$, i.e. for every vector $\boldsymbol{a}$ there exist such three numbers α_1, α_2, and α_3 that

$$\boldsymbol{a} = \alpha_1 \boldsymbol{e}_1 + \alpha_2 \boldsymbol{e}_2 + \alpha_3 \boldsymbol{e}_3 . \tag{31}$$

(ii) The coefficients α_1, α_2, and α_3 of this linear combination are defined uniquely for any given $\boldsymbol{a}$.

The proofs of these statements are analogous to the proofs of the statements of Theorem 1.4.3.

Let us translate (if necessary) vectors $\boldsymbol{e}_1, \boldsymbol{e}_2, \boldsymbol{e}_3$, and $\boldsymbol{a}$ so as to make their origins to be located at the same point, labeled O.

If vector $\boldsymbol{a}$ is coplanar with $\boldsymbol{e}_1$ and $\boldsymbol{e}_2$, then it is their linear combination (by Theorem 1.4.3): $\boldsymbol{a} = \alpha_1 \boldsymbol{e}_1 + \alpha_2 \boldsymbol{e}_2$. In this case we can write

$$\boldsymbol{a} = \alpha_1 \boldsymbol{e}_1 + \alpha_2 \boldsymbol{e}_2 + 0 \cdot \boldsymbol{e}_3 , \tag{32}$$

which means that $\boldsymbol{a}$ is a linear combination of $\boldsymbol{e}_1$, $\boldsymbol{e}_2$, and $\boldsymbol{e}_3$, and the coefficients of this combination are defined uniquely (why?), so the statement is proved.

If vector $\boldsymbol{a}$ is not coplanar with $\boldsymbol{e}_1$ and $\boldsymbol{e}_2$, we shall draw through its endpoint A a line parallel to vector $\boldsymbol{e}_3$ (Figure 15). Since $\boldsymbol{e}_3$ is not coplanar with $\boldsymbol{e}_1$ and $\boldsymbol{e}_2$, this line will intersect plane P, in which $\boldsymbol{e}_1$ and $\boldsymbol{e}_2$ lie, at some point B.

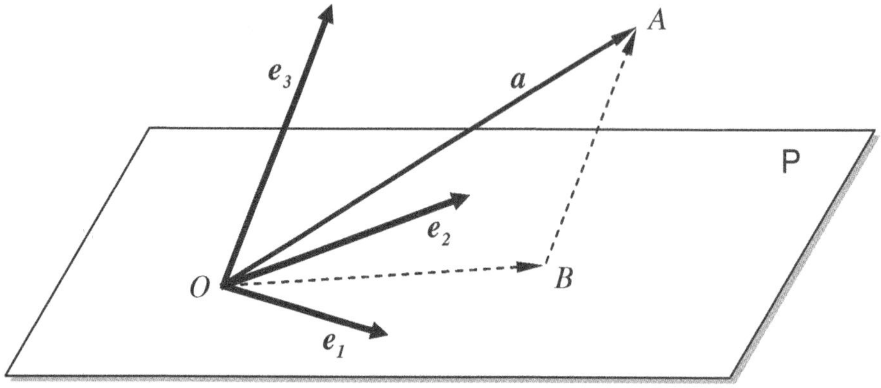

Figure 15

Then vector $\boldsymbol{a} = \overrightarrow{OA}$ is a sum of two vectors:

$$\boldsymbol{a} = \overrightarrow{OA} = \overrightarrow{OB} + \overrightarrow{BA}. \qquad (33)$$

The first of these vectors, vector $\overrightarrow{OB}$, lies in plane P, and therefore, according to Theorem 1.4.3, it is a linear combination of vectors $\boldsymbol{e}_1$ and $\boldsymbol{e}_2$:

$$\overrightarrow{OB} = \alpha_1\boldsymbol{e}_1 + \alpha_2\boldsymbol{e}_2, \qquad (34)$$

whose coefficients α_1 and α_2 are defined uniquely.

The second vector of the sum, vector $\overrightarrow{BA}$, is collinear with $\boldsymbol{e}_3$, and is therefore its multiple:

$$\overrightarrow{BA} = \alpha_3\boldsymbol{e}_3, \qquad (35)$$

where the coefficient α_3 is defined uniquely (Theorem 1.3.1).

By substituting these expressions for $\overrightarrow{OB}$ and $\overrightarrow{BA}$ into (33), we obtain

$$\boldsymbol{a} = \alpha_1\boldsymbol{e}_1 + \alpha_2\boldsymbol{e}_2 + \alpha_n\boldsymbol{e}_3, \qquad (36)$$

where the coefficients α_1, α_2, and α_3 are defined uniquely. □

Based on this result we can say than any three noncoplanar vectors taken in a certain order, form a basis in the space of geometric vectors:

Definition. Any ordered triple of noncoplanar vectors $\boldsymbol{e}_1, \boldsymbol{e}_2, \boldsymbol{e}_3$ is a *basis* in the space of geometric vectors. If $\boldsymbol{a} = \alpha_1\boldsymbol{e}_1 + \alpha_2\boldsymbol{e}_2 + \alpha_n\boldsymbol{e}_3$, this expression is called *the expansion of* $\boldsymbol{a}$ *in the basis* $\{\boldsymbol{e}_1, \boldsymbol{e}_2, \boldsymbol{e}_3\}$, and the coefficients of this linear combination are called the *coordinates* (or *components*) of $\boldsymbol{a}$ in the basis $\{\boldsymbol{e}_1, \boldsymbol{e}_2, \boldsymbol{e}_3\}$.

Similarly to the case of a plane of vectors, we can define the space of ordered triples of numbers R^3 and show that there is an *isomorphism* between this space and the space of geometric vectors. The proofs are almost identical to the corresponding proofs for R^2, and we omit them.

Definition. *Arithmetic space* R^3 is the set of all ordered triples of numbers (or 3-columns), for which the operations of addition and multiplication by numbers are defined as follows:

$$\begin{bmatrix}\alpha_1\\ \alpha_2\\ \alpha_3\end{bmatrix}+\begin{bmatrix}\beta_1\\ \beta_2\\ \beta_3\end{bmatrix}=\begin{bmatrix}\alpha_1+\beta_1\\ \alpha_2+\beta_2\\ \alpha_3+\beta_3\end{bmatrix};\quad k\begin{bmatrix}\alpha_1\\ \alpha_2\\ \alpha_3\end{bmatrix}=\begin{bmatrix}k\alpha_1\\ k\alpha_2\\ k\alpha_3\end{bmatrix}. \tag{37}$$

One can show that these operations possess all the properties (1-8) of linear operations with vectors.

Theorem 1.4.12 The space of geometric vectors is isomorphic to R^3: for any given basis $\{\boldsymbol{e}_1, \boldsymbol{e}_2, \boldsymbol{e}_3\}$ there is a one-to-one correspondence between the vectors and the respective columns of their components:

$$\boldsymbol{a}=\alpha_1\boldsymbol{e}_1+\alpha_2\boldsymbol{e}_2+\alpha_3\boldsymbol{e}_3 \quad \leftrightarrow \quad \begin{bmatrix}\alpha_1\\ \alpha_2\\ \alpha_3\end{bmatrix}, \tag{38}$$

and this correspondence is preserved by linear operations.
In this connection, the vectors of the basis $\{\boldsymbol{e}_1, \boldsymbol{e}_2, \boldsymbol{e}_3\}$ in the space of vectors are in correspondence with the respective vectors

$$\left\{\begin{bmatrix}1\\ 0\\ 0\end{bmatrix}, \begin{bmatrix}0\\ 1\\ 0\end{bmatrix}, \begin{bmatrix}1\\ 0\\ 1\end{bmatrix}\right\} \tag{39}$$

that constitute the standard basis in R^3.

In the future we shall identify the geometric vectors with their respective columns and write

$$\boldsymbol{a}=\begin{bmatrix}\alpha_1\\ \alpha_2\\ \alpha_3\end{bmatrix}. \tag{40}$$

When writing such an equality, we should always keep in mind that a certain basis is identified with the standard basis in R^3.

The isomorphism we have established allows us to propose simple algebraic solutions to complicated geometric problems. Let us consider an example of such a problem.

Example 5. Let $\{\boldsymbol{i},\boldsymbol{j},\boldsymbol{k}\}$ be a basis in the space of geometric vectors. Determine if the vectors $\boldsymbol{u}=\boldsymbol{i}-\boldsymbol{j}-2\boldsymbol{k}$, $\boldsymbol{v}=\boldsymbol{j}+\boldsymbol{k}$, and $\boldsymbol{w}=-\boldsymbol{i}+2\boldsymbol{j}+3\boldsymbol{k}$ are a basis in this space.

Solution. Three vectors are a basis if they are noncoplanar, which is difficult to check geometrically. Let us solve the problem algebraically. We know that three vectors are noncoplanar if and only if they are linearly independent. Let us check if the given three vectors are linearly independent. It is so if

$$x_1\boldsymbol{u}+x_2\boldsymbol{v}+x_3\boldsymbol{w}=\boldsymbol{0} \tag{41}$$

only when

$$x_1=x_2=x_3=0\,. \tag{42}$$

For convenience, we suggest that the basis $\{\boldsymbol{i},\boldsymbol{j},\boldsymbol{k}\}$ correspond to the standard basis (39) in R^3. Then the condition (41) can be written as

$$x_1\begin{bmatrix}1\\-1\\-2\end{bmatrix}+x_2\begin{bmatrix}0\\1\\1\end{bmatrix}+x_3\begin{bmatrix}-1\\2\\3\end{bmatrix}=\begin{bmatrix}0\\0\\0\end{bmatrix}, \tag{43}$$

which after performing the operations with columns can be written as

$$\begin{bmatrix}x_1 \quad -x_3\\-x_1+x_2+2x_3\\-2x_1+x_2+3x_3\end{bmatrix}=\begin{bmatrix}0\\0\\0\end{bmatrix} \quad\Rightarrow\quad \begin{cases}x_1 \quad -x_3=0\\-x_1+x_2+2x_3=0\\-2x_1+x_2+3x_3=0\end{cases} \tag{44}$$

This system of equations can be solved by the procedure called Gaussian elimination. First, we shall eliminate the first variable x_1 from the second and third equations: we shall add the first equation to the second, and add the first equation multiplied by 2 to the third one:

$$\begin{cases}x_1 \quad -x_3=0\\-x_1+x_2+2x_3=0\\-2x_1+x_2+3x_3=0\end{cases}\rightarrow\begin{pmatrix}\\E2\rightarrow E2+E1\\E3\rightarrow E3+2\cdot E1\end{pmatrix}\rightarrow\begin{cases}x_1 \quad -x_3=0\\x_2+x_3=0.\\x_2+x_3=0\end{cases} \tag{45}$$

In the next step of solution we should eliminate x_2 from the third equation by subtracting the second equation from the third one. This leads to the system

$$\begin{cases}x_1 \quad -x_3=0\\x_2+x_3=0,\\0=0\end{cases} \tag{46}$$

which has infinitely many solutions: if we take $x_1=x_3$ and $x_2=-x_3$, such a set $(x_1,x_2,x_3)=(x_3,-x_3,x_3)$ will be a solution of the system for any given x_3. If we denote x_3 by a single symbol t, the *general solution* of the system can be written as

$$\begin{cases} x_1 = t \\ x_2 = -t, \\ x_3 = t \end{cases} \tag{47}$$

where t is any real number.

In our particular problem, it is important that t does not have to be zero, and the system has a *non-zero* (also called *nontrivial*) solution, i.e. a solution that does not consist entirely of zeros. If, for instance, $t=1$, then $x_1 = 1; x_2 = -1; x_3 = 1$, and equation (41) can be written for this *particular solution* as

$$\boldsymbol{u} - \boldsymbol{v} + \boldsymbol{w} = \boldsymbol{0}, \tag{48}$$

which means that the vectors $\boldsymbol{u}$, $\boldsymbol{v}$, and $\boldsymbol{w}$ are linearly dependent and therefore they are not a basis.

The last relation and the conclusion have not been obtained for geometrical vectors, but for their column counterparts; it is due to the existing isomorphism that we can extend the conclusion concerning R^3 to the space of geometric vectors. □

The space of points (*affine space*) and the *associated vector space* can be considered analogously to our treatment of a plane of points and the *associated* plane of vectors. We shall introduce Cartesian coordinate systems and describe the basic results without proving any since all the proofs would repeat the ones for the planes.

We can construct a Cartesian coordinate system in space by translating the vectors of a basis to a common point, called the origin, and associating a coordinate axis with each vector of the basis (Figure 16).

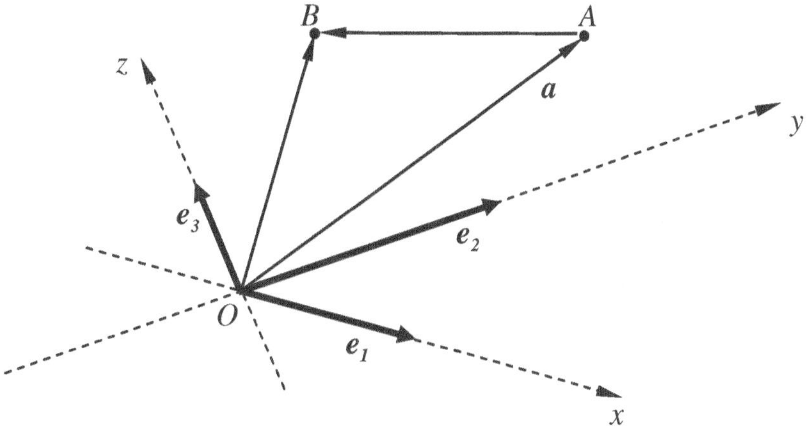

Figure 16

Each point of the space is assigned its position vector, and the coordinates of this vector are by definition the *Cartesian* (*affine*) *coordinates* of the point.

For example (Figure 16), if the expansion of vector $\overrightarrow{OA} = \boldsymbol{a}$ in some basis $\{\boldsymbol{e}_1, \boldsymbol{e}_2, \boldsymbol{e}_3\}$ is $\boldsymbol{a} = \alpha_1 \boldsymbol{e}_1 + \alpha_2 \boldsymbol{e}_2 + \alpha_n \boldsymbol{e}_3$, and a Cartesian coordinate system is built upon this basis, then the coordinates of point A will be

$$(x_A, y_A, z_A) = (\alpha_1, \alpha_2, \alpha_3). \quad (49)$$

Also, for every pair of points in (affine) space we can assign a vector, whose coordinates are determined by the coordinates of these points as stated in the following theorem.

Theorem 1.4.13 If A and B are two points in a Cartesian plane , and their respective coordinates are (x_A, y_A, z_A) and (x_B, y_B, z_B), then the coordinates of the vector $\overrightarrow{AB}$ connecting these points are $(x_B - x_A, y_B - y_A, z_B - z_A)$.

Since R^3 is isomorphic to the space of vectors, we can consider R^3 as the space associated with the space of points. We shall do this by assigning each point a 3-column whose entries are the respective coordinates of the position vector of the point in a given basis.

PRACTICE PROBLEMS (Section1: Linear Operations with Geometric Vectors)

1. Prove property 7 (distributive law: $(\alpha + \beta)\boldsymbol{a} = \alpha\boldsymbol{a} + \beta\boldsymbol{a}$) of linear operations with geometric vectors (this is an advanced problem, the proof is rather lengthy and may be omitted in the first reading).

2. Use the properties of linear operations with vectors to prove that for any vector $\boldsymbol{a}$, $(-1)\boldsymbol{a} = -\boldsymbol{a}$.

3. For the given vectors $\boldsymbol{a}$ and $\boldsymbol{b}$ (see the figure below), construct the following vectors: $\boldsymbol{a} - \boldsymbol{b}$, $2\boldsymbol{a} + \boldsymbol{b}$, $3\boldsymbol{b} - \frac{1}{2}\boldsymbol{a}$.

Figure 1

4. In the figure below, $ABCDEF$ is a regular hexagon with the centre at O. Given that $\vec{FA} = \boldsymbol{u}$, and $\vec{OD} = \boldsymbol{v}$, express vectors $\vec{FB}$ and $\vec{FC}$ as linear combinations of $\boldsymbol{u}$ and $\boldsymbol{v}$.

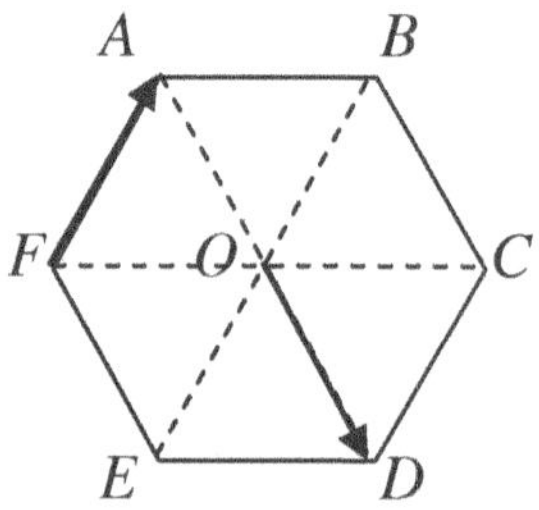

Figure 2

5. In Figure 3, $ABCD$ is a square, O is its centre, and M and N are the midpoints of AD and DC. $\overrightarrow{DN} = \boldsymbol{i}$; $\overrightarrow{DM} = \boldsymbol{j}$. Determine the coordinates (components) of vector $\overrightarrow{AC}$

in the basis $\{\boldsymbol{i}, \boldsymbol{j}\}$;

in the basis $\{\overrightarrow{CO}, \overrightarrow{AB}\}$;

in the basis $\{\overrightarrow{MC}, \boldsymbol{j}\}$

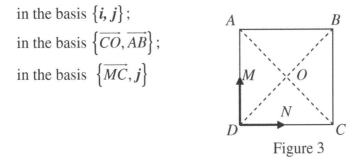

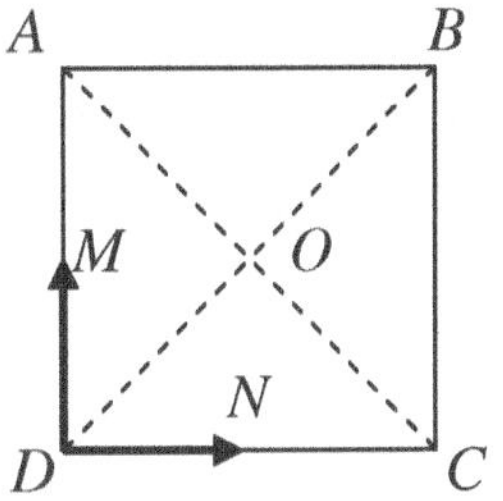

Figure 3

6. Vectors $\boldsymbol{a}$ and $\boldsymbol{b}$ are given: $\boldsymbol{a} = -\boldsymbol{i} + 2\boldsymbol{j}$ and $\boldsymbol{b} = 3\boldsymbol{i} - 6\boldsymbol{j}$.
determine if they form a basis in the plane;
determine if the vector $\boldsymbol{v} = -4\boldsymbol{i} + 8\boldsymbol{j}$ is in their spanning set.

7. $\boldsymbol{u} = \begin{bmatrix} 1 \\ 3 \end{bmatrix}$, and $\boldsymbol{v} = \begin{bmatrix} -1 \\ 2 \end{bmatrix}$.

Determine if these vectors form a basis in R^2.

If they do, find the components of $\boldsymbol{a} = \begin{bmatrix} 3 \\ 4 \end{bmatrix}$ in their basis.

8. $\boldsymbol{u} = \begin{bmatrix} 1 \\ -1 \\ 2 \end{bmatrix}$, $\boldsymbol{v} = \begin{bmatrix} 0 \\ 3 \\ 1 \end{bmatrix}$, and $\boldsymbol{w} = \begin{bmatrix} -2 \\ 5 \\ -3 \end{bmatrix}$.

Determine if these vectors form a basis in R^3.

Does vector $\boldsymbol{a} = \begin{bmatrix} 2 \\ 1 \\ 5 \end{bmatrix}$ belong to Span $\{\boldsymbol{u}, \boldsymbol{v}, \boldsymbol{w}\}$?

9. $\boldsymbol{e}_1 = \begin{bmatrix} 1 \\ -1 \\ 0 \end{bmatrix}$, $\boldsymbol{e}_2 = \begin{bmatrix} 1 \\ 1 \\ 1 \end{bmatrix}$, and $\boldsymbol{e}_3 = \begin{bmatrix} 0 \\ 1 \\ 1 \end{bmatrix}$.

(a) Determine if these vectors form a basis in R^3.
(b) If they do form a basis, find the components of the vector

$\boldsymbol{a} = \begin{bmatrix} 3 \\ 0 \\ 5 \end{bmatrix}$ in their basis.

10. Points A and B are given by they coordinates in a Cartesian rectangular system: $A(1, -1, 3)$; $B(7, 8, 12)$. Find the coordinates of such a point M located on the segment AB that $AM : MB = 3{:}5$.

SOLUTIONS TO PRACTICE PROBLEMS (Section 1)

1. Prove property 7 (distributive law: $(\alpha+\beta)\boldsymbol{a} = \alpha\boldsymbol{a} + \beta\boldsymbol{a}$) of linear operations with geometric vectors.

Solution. In order to prove the property we have to show that the vectors $\boldsymbol{u} = (\alpha+\beta)\boldsymbol{a}$ and $\boldsymbol{v} = \alpha\boldsymbol{a} + \beta\boldsymbol{a}$ (a) have the same length (norm) and (b) are parallel (collinear and co-directed).

It follows directly from the definition of scalar multiplication that all the participating vectors, namely $(\alpha+\beta)\boldsymbol{a}$, $\alpha\boldsymbol{a}$, and $\beta\boldsymbol{a}$ are collinear with $\boldsymbol{a}$, and therefore they are collinear with each other. Also, the sum of two collinear vectors will join the origin of the first vector with the terminal point of the second, and thus it will lie on the same line as the addends that make this sum (there is one and only one line through any pair of points!). Hence, the vectors $\boldsymbol{u}$ and $\boldsymbol{v}$ are collinear. Each of them may be parallel (co-directed) or antiparallel (oppositely directed) to $\boldsymbol{a}$ depending on the signs and magnitudes of α and β.

Therefore we shall have to consider all possible cases involving various signs and relative values of α and β. Before we start doing this, let us make an important observation concerning the lengths of sums of collinear vectors:

(i) If two vectors, $\boldsymbol{p}$ and $\boldsymbol{q}$, are parallel (collinear and co-directed), the length of their sum is equal the sum of their lengths: $\|\boldsymbol{p}+\boldsymbol{q}\| = \|\boldsymbol{p}\| + \|\boldsymbol{q}\|$ (see Figure (i) below).

(ii) If two vectors, $\boldsymbol{p}$ and $\boldsymbol{q}$, are antiparallel (collinear and oppositely directed), the length of their sum is equal the absolute value of the difference between their lengths: $\|\boldsymbol{p}+\boldsymbol{q}\| = \big|\,\|\boldsymbol{p}\| - \|\boldsymbol{q}\|\,\big|$ (see Figure (ii) below, in which $\boldsymbol{q}$ is longer than $\boldsymbol{p}$, so $\big|\,\|\boldsymbol{p}\| - \|\boldsymbol{q}\|\,\big| = \|\boldsymbol{q}\| - \|\boldsymbol{p}\|$).

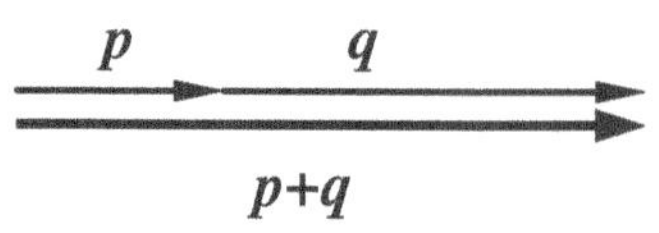

(i)

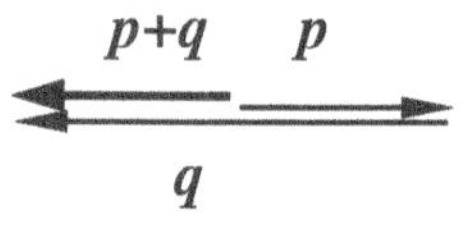

(ii)

Now let us consider all possible situations.

(a) $\alpha > 0$; $\beta > 0$.

In this case the vectors $(\alpha+\beta)\boldsymbol{a}$, $\alpha\boldsymbol{a}$, and $\beta\boldsymbol{a}$ are all parallel (co-directed) to $\boldsymbol{a}$. Since $\alpha\boldsymbol{a}$ and $\beta\boldsymbol{a}$ are co-directed,

$\|\alpha\boldsymbol{a}+\beta\boldsymbol{a}\| = (\text{according to the case (i) of the above remark}) = \|\alpha\boldsymbol{a}\| + \|\beta\boldsymbol{a}\| =$

$= |\alpha|\|\boldsymbol{a}\| + |\beta|\|\boldsymbol{a}\| = (|\alpha|+|\beta|)\|\boldsymbol{a}\| = |\alpha+\beta|\|\boldsymbol{a}\|.$

On the other hand, $\|(\alpha+\beta)\boldsymbol{a}\| = (\text{by definition}) = |\alpha+\beta|\|\boldsymbol{a}\|$.

Therefore the lengths (norms) of the vectors $\boldsymbol{u} = (\alpha+\beta)\boldsymbol{a}$ and $\boldsymbol{v} = \alpha\boldsymbol{a}+\beta\boldsymbol{a}$ are equal; also they are parallel, since each of them is co-directed with $\boldsymbol{a}$; hence these vectors are equal.

(b) $\alpha > 0; \beta < 0$.

First let us consider the case when $|\alpha| > |\beta|$.

In this case, $\boldsymbol{u} = (\alpha+\beta)\boldsymbol{a} = (\alpha-|\beta|)\boldsymbol{a}$ is a vector parallel to $\boldsymbol{a}$, and its length is equal $\|\boldsymbol{u}\| = \|(\alpha-|\beta|)\boldsymbol{a}\| = (\alpha-|\beta|)\|\boldsymbol{a}\|$ (draw the diagram that illustrates this).

Vector $\boldsymbol{v}$ will be parallel to a as well (draw the respective diagram), and, according to the case (ii) of the above remark,

$\|\boldsymbol{v}\| = \|\alpha\boldsymbol{a}+\beta\boldsymbol{a}\| = |\,\|\alpha\boldsymbol{a}\| - \|\beta\boldsymbol{a}\|\,| = |\,\alpha\|\boldsymbol{a}\| - |\beta|\|\boldsymbol{a}\|\,| = |\alpha-|\beta||\|\boldsymbol{a}\| = (\alpha-|\beta|)\|\boldsymbol{a}\|.$

Hence the two vectors are equal.

It is easy to see that in case when $|\alpha| > |\beta|$, each of the vectors $\boldsymbol{u}$ and $\boldsymbol{v}$ will be antiparallel to $\boldsymbol{a}$, and their lengths will be equal to the same value $(|\beta|-\alpha)\|\boldsymbol{a}\|$, and therefore they are equal in this case as well.

(c) $\alpha < 0; \beta > 0$.

The proof will just repeat the above one with α and β interchanged.

(d) $\alpha < 0; \beta < 0$.

Since each of the vectors $(\alpha+\beta)\boldsymbol{a}$, $\alpha\boldsymbol{a}$, and $\beta\boldsymbol{a}$ is antiparallel to $\boldsymbol{a}$, both $\boldsymbol{u}$ and $\boldsymbol{v}$ will be antiparallel to $\boldsymbol{a}$. Since $\alpha\boldsymbol{a}$ and $\beta\boldsymbol{a}$ are parallel (co-directed), the treatment of the lengths of $\boldsymbol{u}$ and $\boldsymbol{v}$ is exactly the same as for the case when $\alpha > 0; \beta > 0$ (let us notice that for both negative numbers the sum of their absolute values is equal to the absolute value of their sum: $|\alpha|+|\beta| = -\alpha-\beta = -(\alpha+\beta) = |\alpha+\beta|$). Therefore,

$\|\alpha\boldsymbol{a}+\beta\boldsymbol{a}\| = (\text{according to the case (i) of the above remark}) = \|\alpha\boldsymbol{a}\| + \|\beta\boldsymbol{a}\| =$

$= |\alpha|\|\boldsymbol{a}\| + |\beta|\|\boldsymbol{a}\| = (|\alpha|+|\beta|)\|\boldsymbol{a}\| = |\alpha+\beta|\|\boldsymbol{a}\|.$

On the other hand, $\|(\alpha+\beta)\boldsymbol{a}\| = (\text{by definition}) = |\alpha+\beta|\|\boldsymbol{a}\|$.

Hence, the lengths (norms) of the vectors $\boldsymbol{u} = (\alpha+\beta)\boldsymbol{a}$ and $\boldsymbol{v} = \alpha\boldsymbol{a}+\beta\boldsymbol{a}$ are equal; also they are parallel, since each of them is antiparallel to $\boldsymbol{a}$; so these vectors are equal. This completes the proof. □

2. Use the properties of linear operations with vectors to prove that for any vector $\boldsymbol{a}$, $(-1)\boldsymbol{a} = -\boldsymbol{a}$.

Solution. By definition, a vector is said to be an opposite of $\boldsymbol{a}$ if its sum with $\boldsymbol{a}$ is $\boldsymbol{0}$. Thus, in order to show that $(-1)\boldsymbol{a}$ is an opposite of $\boldsymbol{a}$, we have to show that $(-1)\boldsymbol{a} + \boldsymbol{a} = \boldsymbol{0}$.

$(-1)\boldsymbol{a} + \boldsymbol{a} = (\text{By property (5)}) = (-1)\boldsymbol{a} + (1)\boldsymbol{a} = (\text{By property (7)}) = [(-1)+1]\boldsymbol{a} = 0\cdot\boldsymbol{a}$.

Now let us show that $0\cdot\boldsymbol{a} = \boldsymbol{0}$.

Let $\boldsymbol{b}$ be an arbitrary vector. Then

$\boldsymbol{b} + 0\cdot\boldsymbol{a} = (\text{By property (4)}) = \boldsymbol{b} + ((-\boldsymbol{a}) + \boldsymbol{a}) + 0\cdot\boldsymbol{a} = (\text{By properties (5)and (2)}) =$

$\boldsymbol{b} + (-\boldsymbol{a}) + ((1)\,\boldsymbol{a} + 0\cdot\boldsymbol{a}) = (\text{By property (7)}) = \boldsymbol{b} + (-\boldsymbol{a}) + (1+0)\boldsymbol{a} = \boldsymbol{b} + (-\boldsymbol{a}) + (1\cdot\boldsymbol{a}) =$

$(\text{By property (5)}) = \boldsymbol{b} + ((-\boldsymbol{a}) + \boldsymbol{a}) = \boldsymbol{b} + \boldsymbol{0}.$

Thus $\boldsymbol{b} + 0\cdot\boldsymbol{a} = \boldsymbol{b} + \boldsymbol{0}$, and by adding $(-\boldsymbol{b})$ to both sides of the latter equality, we obtain: $0\cdot\boldsymbol{a} = \boldsymbol{0}$, which means that $0\cdot\boldsymbol{a}$ is a zero vector.

We have obtained earlier that $(-1)\boldsymbol{a} + \boldsymbol{a} = 0\cdot\boldsymbol{a}$; hence, $(-1)\boldsymbol{a} + \boldsymbol{a} = \boldsymbol{0}$, which completes the proof.

Let us notice that in this proof we did not use the fact that we are dealing with geometric vectors: the proof has been based exclusively on the properties of linear operations. It is important since it shows the validity of the statement for *any* kind of vectors as long as we mean by vectors a set of objects with two operations possessing the properties (1-8).

3. For the given vectors $\boldsymbol{a}$ and $\boldsymbol{b}$ (see the figure below), construct the following vectors: $\boldsymbol{a} - \boldsymbol{b}$, $2\boldsymbol{a} + \boldsymbol{b}$, $3\boldsymbol{b} - \frac{1}{2}\boldsymbol{a}$.

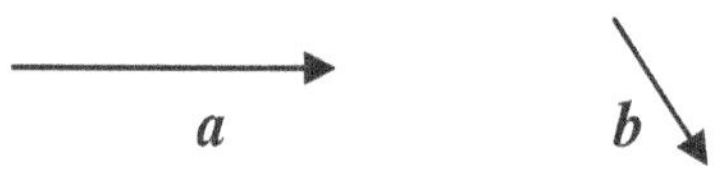

Figure 1

Solution. The solutions are shown in dotted lines in the diagram below.

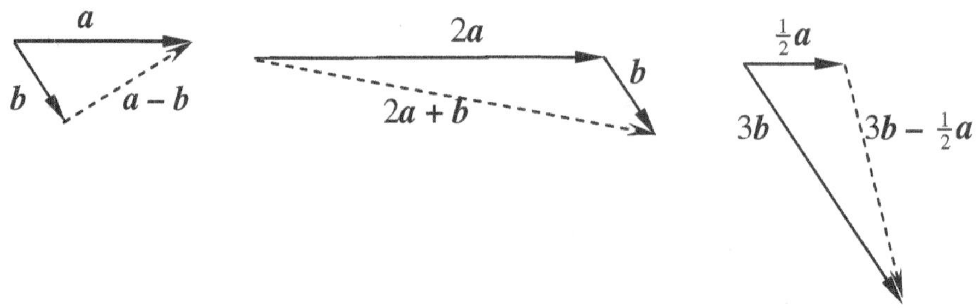

4. In the figure below, $ABCDEF$ is a regular hexagon with the centre at O. Given that $\vec{FA} = \boldsymbol{u}$, and $\vec{OD} = \boldsymbol{v}$, express vectors $\vec{FB}$ and $\vec{FC}$ as linear combinations of $\boldsymbol{u}$ and $\boldsymbol{v}$.

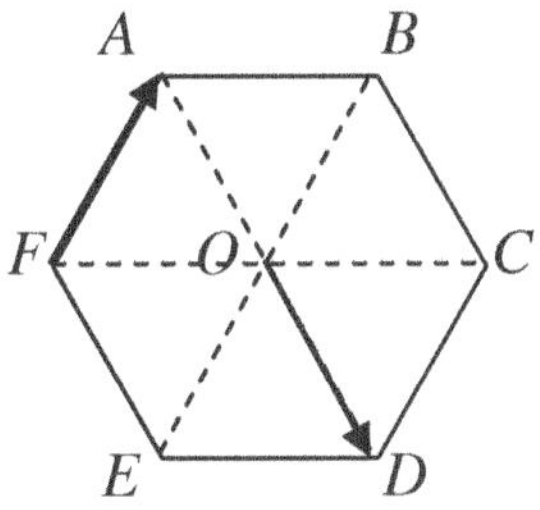

Figure 2

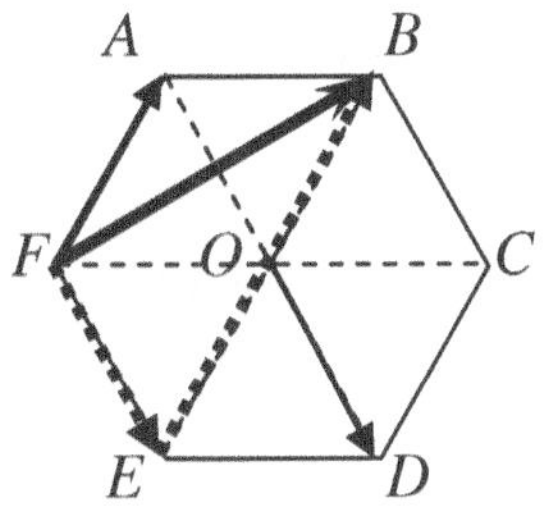

Figure(a)

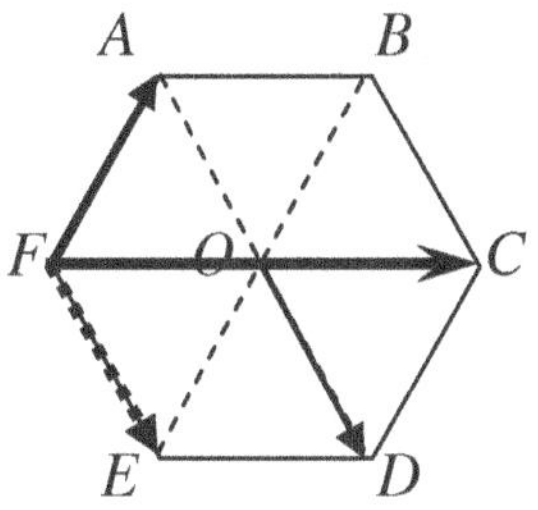

Figure(b)

Solution. In Figure (a), $\overrightarrow{FB} = \overrightarrow{FE} + \overrightarrow{EB} = \boldsymbol{v} + 2\boldsymbol{u} = 2\boldsymbol{u} + \boldsymbol{v}$.
In Figure (b), $\overrightarrow{FC} = 2\overrightarrow{FO} = 2\left(\overrightarrow{FA} + \overrightarrow{FE}\right) = 2\left(\overrightarrow{FA} + \overrightarrow{OD}\right) = 2(\boldsymbol{u} + \boldsymbol{v}) = 2\boldsymbol{u} + 2\boldsymbol{v}$.
There are many other ways of expressing these vectors as linear combinations of $\boldsymbol{u}$ and $\boldsymbol{v}$, yet the answers will be the same. – Why?

5. In Figure 3, $ABCD$ is a square, O is its centre, and M and N are the midpoints of AD and DC. $\overrightarrow{DN} = \boldsymbol{i}$; $\overrightarrow{DM} = \boldsymbol{j}$. Determine the coordinates (components) of vector $\overrightarrow{AC}$

(i) in the basis $\{\boldsymbol{i}, \boldsymbol{j}\}$;

(ii) in the basis $\{\overrightarrow{CO}, \overrightarrow{AB}\}$;

(iii) in the basis $\{\overrightarrow{MC}, \boldsymbol{j}\}$

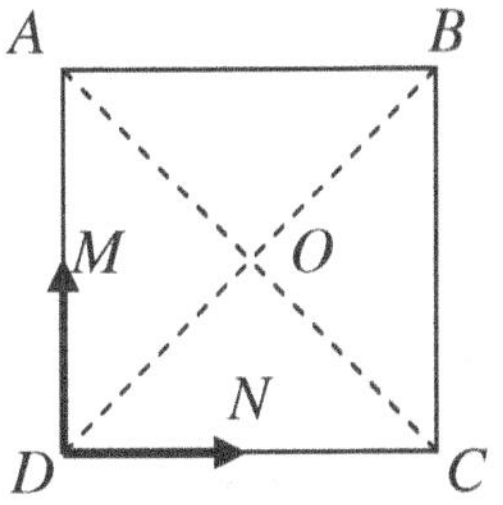

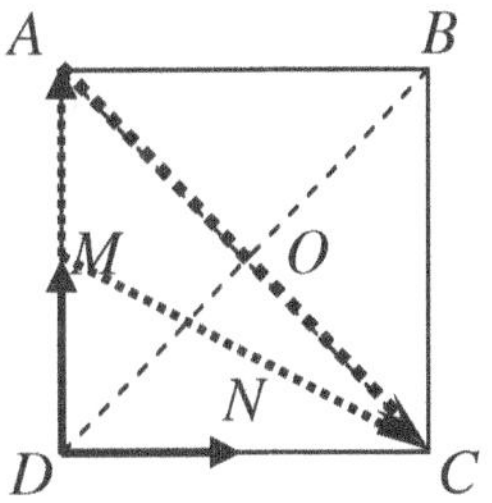

Figure 3

Solution.
(i) $\overrightarrow{AC} = \overrightarrow{DC} - \overrightarrow{DA} = 2\boldsymbol{i} - 2\boldsymbol{j}$; the coordinates are (2, –2).
(ii) $\overrightarrow{AC} = (-2)\overrightarrow{CO} = (-2) \cdot \overrightarrow{CO} + 0 \cdot \overrightarrow{AB}$; the coordinates are (–2, 0).
(iii) It is easy to see at the diagram above that $\overrightarrow{MA} + \overrightarrow{AC} = \overrightarrow{MC}$, whence $\overrightarrow{AC} = \overrightarrow{MC} - \overrightarrow{MA} = \overrightarrow{MC} - \boldsymbol{j} = 1 \cdot \overrightarrow{MC} + (-1) \cdot \boldsymbol{j}$, i.e. the coordinates are (1, –1).

6. Vectors $\boldsymbol{a}$ and $\boldsymbol{b}$ are given: $\boldsymbol{a} = -\boldsymbol{i} + 2\boldsymbol{j}$ and $\boldsymbol{b} = 3\boldsymbol{i} - 6\boldsymbol{j}$.

(a) determine if they form a basis in a plane that contains them;

(b) determine if vector $\boldsymbol{v} = -4\boldsymbol{i} + 8\boldsymbol{j}$ is in their spanning set.

<u>Solution.</u> It is interesting to see how this problem can be solved in a few different ways. Each solution, of course, leads to the same answers.

<u>Solution 1 (the easiest).</u>

(a) Two vectors are a basis in the plane iff (if and only if) they are not collinear. Let us check if they are collinear. They are collinear iff they are proportional, i.e. one of them is a multiple of the other. It is the case iff there exists such a number x that $\boldsymbol{b} = x\boldsymbol{a}$.

For our particular vectors this equality can be written as $3\boldsymbol{i} - 6\boldsymbol{j} = x(-\boldsymbol{i} + 2\boldsymbol{j})$.

The latter equality can be rewritten as $3\boldsymbol{i} - 6\boldsymbol{j} = -x\boldsymbol{i} + 2x\boldsymbol{j}$, which leads (try to explain why) to the system of simultaneous equations

$\begin{cases} -x = 3 \\ 2x = -6 \end{cases}$, which has a solution $x = -3$.

Thus, $\boldsymbol{b} = -3\boldsymbol{a}$, which means that $\boldsymbol{a}$ and $\boldsymbol{b}$ are collinear and hence they do not form a basis in V^2.

(b) Even though these two vectors are not a basis, they still can span some vectors, only those that are collinear with them (Theorem 2). Let us check if $\boldsymbol{v}$ is collinear with $\boldsymbol{a}$ (or $\boldsymbol{b}$). It is easy to find that $\boldsymbol{v} = 4\boldsymbol{a}$, i.e. $\boldsymbol{v}$ is collinear with $\boldsymbol{a}$ (and , of course, with $\boldsymbol{b}$ as well), therefore $\boldsymbol{v}$ is a linear combination of $\boldsymbol{a}$ and $\boldsymbol{b}$: we can write the latter equality as $\boldsymbol{v} = 4 \cdot \boldsymbol{a} + 0 \cdot \boldsymbol{b}$; hence $\boldsymbol{v} \in Span\{\boldsymbol{a}, \boldsymbol{b}\}$.

<u>Solution 2 (the most general, - a similar approach will solve problems of this kind in any space, not only in a plane of vectors).</u>

(a) Two vectors are a basis in the plane iff every vector of the plane is their linear combination. Let vector $\boldsymbol{r} = x\boldsymbol{i} + y\boldsymbol{j}$ be an arbitrary vector of the plane. In order to solve the problem we shall find out if this vector can be presented as a linear combination of $\boldsymbol{a}$ and $\boldsymbol{b}$ for any numbers x and y.

In other words, let us find out if there exist such numbers α and β that $\boldsymbol{r} = \alpha\boldsymbol{a} + \beta\boldsymbol{b}$.

The latter equality means: $\alpha(-\boldsymbol{i} + 2\boldsymbol{j}) + \beta(3\boldsymbol{i} - 6\boldsymbol{j}) = x\boldsymbol{i} + y\boldsymbol{j}$, or

$(-\alpha + 3\beta)\boldsymbol{i} + (2\alpha - 6\beta)\boldsymbol{j} = x\boldsymbol{i} + y\boldsymbol{j}$. Since $\boldsymbol{i}$ and $\boldsymbol{j}$ form a basis in V^2, the coordinates of the vectors in the left-hand and right-hand sides of this equations must be equal, which leads to the system:

$$\begin{cases} -\alpha + 3\beta = x \\ 2\alpha - 6\beta = y \end{cases} \rightarrow (E_2 \rightarrow E_2 + 2E_1) \rightarrow \begin{cases} -\alpha + 3\beta & = & x \\ 0 & = & y + 2x \end{cases}$$

The latter system has solutions only if $y + 2x = 0$ (otherwise the second equation will be a false identity). Hence, only those vectors $\boldsymbol{r} = x\boldsymbol{i} + y\boldsymbol{j}$ whose components satisfy the equation $x - 2y = 0$ can be spanned by $\boldsymbol{a}$ and $\boldsymbol{b}$. Therefore $\boldsymbol{a}$ and $\boldsymbol{b}$ do not form a basis in V^2.

(b) The components of $\boldsymbol{v} = -4\boldsymbol{i} + 8\boldsymbol{j}$ do satisfy the condition $y + 2x = 0$. Really, $y + 2x = 8 + 2(-4) = 0$, therefore $\boldsymbol{v}$ is a linear combination of $\boldsymbol{a}$ and $\boldsymbol{b}$, or in other words, $\boldsymbol{v} \in Span\{\boldsymbol{a}, \boldsymbol{b}\}$.

7. $\boldsymbol{u} = \begin{bmatrix} 1 \\ 3 \end{bmatrix}$, and $\boldsymbol{v} = \begin{bmatrix} -1 \\ 2 \end{bmatrix}$.

(a) Determine if these vectors form a basis in R^2.

(b) If they do, find the components of $\boldsymbol{a} = \begin{bmatrix} 3 \\ 4 \end{bmatrix}$ in their basis.

Solution. Let us try to answer both questions simultaneously. We can do this by checking whether $\boldsymbol{a}$ is a linear combination of $\boldsymbol{u}$ and $\boldsymbol{v}$. We can encounter only the following three situations:

(i) $\boldsymbol{a}$ is a uniquely defined linear combination of $\boldsymbol{u}$ and $\boldsymbol{v}$, then $\boldsymbol{u}$ and $\boldsymbol{v}$ are a basis in R^2, and the coefficients of the linear combination are the components of $\boldsymbol{a}$ in this basis.

(ii) $\boldsymbol{a}$ is a linear combination of $\boldsymbol{u}$ and $\boldsymbol{v}$, but the coefficients of the combination are not defined uniquely. Then these vectors are not a basis. This situation corresponds to having two collinear vectors that span another vector collinear with them in V^2.

(iii) $\boldsymbol{a}$ is not a linear combination of $\boldsymbol{u}$ and $\boldsymbol{v}$; then they are not a basis in R^2.

Suppose $\boldsymbol{a} = x_1\boldsymbol{u} + x_2\boldsymbol{v}$; then $x_1 \begin{bmatrix} 1 \\ 3 \end{bmatrix} + x_2 \begin{bmatrix} -1 \\ 2 \end{bmatrix} = \begin{bmatrix} 3 \\ 4 \end{bmatrix} \Rightarrow \begin{cases} x_1 - x_2 &= 3 \\ 3x_1 + 2x_2 &= 4 \end{cases}$

In order to eliminate the first variable x_1 from the second equation, we multiply the first equation by (–3) and add to the second (we can briefly describe this operation as $(E_2 \to E_2 - 3E_1)$). The obtained system will be equivalent to the original one.

$$\begin{cases} x_1 - x_2 &= 3 \\ 5x_2 &= -5 \end{cases} \Rightarrow \begin{cases} x_1 - x_2 &= 3 \\ x_2 &= -1 \end{cases} \Rightarrow \begin{cases} x_1 &= 2 \\ x_2 &= -1 \end{cases}$$

This system has a unique solution, which means that $\boldsymbol{u}$ and $\boldsymbol{v}$ do form a basis and the components of $\boldsymbol{a}$ in this basis are 2 and –1.

8. $\boldsymbol{u} = \begin{bmatrix} 1 \\ -1 \\ 2 \end{bmatrix}$, $\boldsymbol{v} = \begin{bmatrix} 0 \\ 3 \\ 1 \end{bmatrix}$, and $\boldsymbol{w} = \begin{bmatrix} -2 \\ 5 \\ -3 \end{bmatrix}$.

(a) Determine if these vectors form a basis in R^3.

(b) Does vector $\boldsymbol{a} = \begin{bmatrix} 2 \\ 1 \\ 5 \end{bmatrix}$ belong to Span $\{\boldsymbol{u}, \boldsymbol{v}, \boldsymbol{w}\}$?

Solution. Let us consider different methods of solving these problem (it is not necessary, - one solution would suffice, but it helps to get used to the notions and ideas of the subject).

Solution1 (straightforward).

(a) Three vectors form a basis in R^3 iff they are noncoplanar (we should have better said "their corresponding vectors in V^3 are noncoplanar, but identify the two spaces since they are isomorphic by identifying any vector $\boldsymbol{a} = \alpha_1\boldsymbol{e}_1 + \alpha_2\boldsymbol{e}_2 + \alpha_3\boldsymbol{e}_3$ with the corresponding triple of its coordinates $(\alpha_1, \alpha_2, \alpha_3)$ that can be also written as a three-column).

Three vectors are coplanar iff one of them is a linear combination of the other two. For instance, in our case one can easily see that $\boldsymbol{u}$ and $\boldsymbol{v}$ are not collinear (why?), then if (and only if) $\boldsymbol{u}$, $\boldsymbol{v}$, and $\boldsymbol{w}$ are coplanar, $\boldsymbol{w}$ is a linear combination of $\boldsymbol{u}$ and $\boldsymbol{v}$: $\boldsymbol{w} = \alpha_1\boldsymbol{u} + \alpha_2\boldsymbol{v}$, or $\boldsymbol{w} - \alpha_1\boldsymbol{u} - \alpha_2\boldsymbol{v} = \boldsymbol{0}$, which means that the three vectors are linearly dependent: their linear combination with non-zero coefficients is $\boldsymbol{0}$. Thus, three vectors $\boldsymbol{u}$, $\boldsymbol{v}$, and $\boldsymbol{w}$ are coplanar iff they are linearly dependent (otherwise they are noncoplanar and so they do form a basis).

Then let us check if there exist such numbers x_1, x_2, x_3 that at least one of them is not 0, and $x_1\boldsymbol{u} + x_2\boldsymbol{v} + x_3\boldsymbol{w} = \boldsymbol{0}$.

$$x_1\boldsymbol{u} + x_2\boldsymbol{v} + x_n\boldsymbol{w} = \boldsymbol{0} \Rightarrow x_1\begin{bmatrix}1\\-1\\2\end{bmatrix} + x_2\begin{bmatrix}0\\3\\1\end{bmatrix} + x_3\begin{bmatrix}-2\\5\\-3\end{bmatrix} = \begin{bmatrix}0\\0\\0\end{bmatrix} \Rightarrow \begin{cases} x_1 + 0x_2 - 2x_3 &= 0 \\ -x_1 + 3x_2 + 5x_3 &= 0 \Rightarrow \\ 2x_1 + \ x_2 - 3x_3 &= 0 \end{cases}$$

$$\begin{cases} x_1 + 0x_2 - 2x_3 &= 0 \\ 3x_2 + 3x_3 &= 0 \Rightarrow \\ x_2 + x_3 &= 0 \end{cases} \begin{cases} x_1 + 0x_2 - 2x_3 &= 0 \\ x_2 + x_3 &= 0 \Rightarrow \\ 0 &= 0 \end{cases} \begin{cases} x_1 = 2x_3 \\ x_2 = -x_3 \end{cases}, \text{ where } x_3 \in \mathrm{R}.$$

Thus, the third variable x_3 is an arbitrary number and the system has infinitely many solutions. Any solution with $x_3 \neq 0$ will be a non-zero solution. For example, we can choose $x_3 = 1$; then it follows from the formulae for the general solution that $x_1 = 2;\ x_2 = -1$, and $x_1\boldsymbol{u} + x_2\boldsymbol{v} + x_3\boldsymbol{w} = \boldsymbol{0}$ can be written as $2\boldsymbol{u} - \boldsymbol{v} + \boldsymbol{w} = \boldsymbol{0}$.

Hence $\boldsymbol{u}$, $\boldsymbol{v}$, and $\boldsymbol{w}$ are linearly dependent and therefore coplanar; so they do not form a basis in R^3.

(b) Even though they do not form a basis, they span some vectors, - those vectors that are coplanar with them. So we have to check if the given vector a is coplanar with $\boldsymbol{u}$, $\boldsymbol{v}$, and $\boldsymbol{w}$. We can do this in many different ways. The easiest is to check if a is a linear combination of any two noncollinear vectors of $\boldsymbol{u}$, $\boldsymbol{v}$, and $\boldsymbol{w}$. We know that $\boldsymbol{u}$ and $\boldsymbol{v}$ are noncollinear. Then let us determine if there exist such numbers α_1 and α_2 that $\boldsymbol{a} = \alpha_1\boldsymbol{u} + \alpha_2\boldsymbol{v}$. The latter equation can be written as a system:

$$\alpha_1\begin{bmatrix}1\\-1\\2\end{bmatrix}+\alpha_2\begin{bmatrix}0\\3\\1\end{bmatrix}=\begin{bmatrix}2\\1\\5\end{bmatrix}\Rightarrow\begin{cases}\alpha_1+0\alpha_2 &= 2\\ -\alpha_1+3\alpha_2 &= 1\\ 2\alpha_1+\alpha_2 &= 5\end{cases}\Rightarrow\begin{cases}\alpha_1+0\alpha_2 &= 2\\ 3\alpha_2 &= 3\\ \alpha_2 &= 1\end{cases}\Rightarrow\begin{cases}\alpha_1=2\\ \alpha_2=1\end{cases}.$$

It turns out that the system has a solution, which means that $\boldsymbol{a} = 2\boldsymbol{u}+\boldsymbol{v}$, therefore $\boldsymbol{a}\in Span\{\boldsymbol{u},\boldsymbol{v}\}$; $\Rightarrow \boldsymbol{a}\in Span\{\boldsymbol{u},\boldsymbol{v},\boldsymbol{w}\}$.

Let us notice that we could solve a system for finding the coefficients of $\boldsymbol{a}$ as a linear combination of all three vectors ($\boldsymbol{u}$, $\boldsymbol{v}$, and $\boldsymbol{w}$). Such a system would have infinitely many solutions (why?) and the existence of these solutions would also mean that $\boldsymbol{a}\in Span\{\boldsymbol{u},\boldsymbol{v},\boldsymbol{w}\}$.

<u>Solution 2 (a short one).</u>

We can start with the part (b) of the problem: find out if there exist such numbers α_1,α_2, and α_3 that $\boldsymbol{a} = \alpha_1\boldsymbol{u}+\alpha_2\boldsymbol{v}+\alpha_3\boldsymbol{w}$. After solving the system we would find the answer: there are infinitely many such sets $(\alpha_1,\alpha_2,\alpha_3)$. Therefore, we conclude, $\boldsymbol{a}\in Span\{\boldsymbol{u},\boldsymbol{v},\boldsymbol{w}\}$, and $\{\boldsymbol{u},\boldsymbol{v},\boldsymbol{w}\}$ is not a basis: had these three vectors been a basis, the system would have a unique solution.

9. $\boldsymbol{e_1}=\begin{bmatrix}1\\-1\\0\end{bmatrix}$, $\boldsymbol{e_2}=\begin{bmatrix}1\\1\\1\end{bmatrix}$, and $\boldsymbol{e_3}=\begin{bmatrix}0\\1\\1\end{bmatrix}$.

(a) Determine if these vectors form a basis in R^3.

(b) If they do form a basis, find the components of the vector $\boldsymbol{a}=\begin{bmatrix}3\\0\\5\end{bmatrix}$ in their basis.

<u>Solution.</u> Let us try to find out if $\boldsymbol{a}$ is a linear combination of $\boldsymbol{e_1},\boldsymbol{e_2}$, and $\boldsymbol{e_3}$:

$$x_1\boldsymbol{e_1}+x_2\boldsymbol{e_2}+\ldots+x_3\boldsymbol{e_3}=\boldsymbol{a}\Rightarrow x_1\begin{bmatrix}1\\-1\\0\end{bmatrix}+x_2\begin{bmatrix}1\\1\\1\end{bmatrix}+x_3\begin{bmatrix}0\\1\\1\end{bmatrix}=\begin{bmatrix}3\\0\\5\end{bmatrix}\Rightarrow\begin{cases}x_1+x_2 &= 3\\ -x_1+x_2+x_3 &= 0\\ x_2+x_3 &= 5\end{cases}\Rightarrow$$

$$\begin{cases}x_1+x_2 &= 3\\ 2x_2+x_3 &= 3\\ x_2+x_3 &= 5\end{cases}\Rightarrow\begin{cases}x_1+x_2 &= 3\\ 2x_2+x_3 &= 3\\ -x_3 &= -7\end{cases}\Rightarrow\begin{cases}x_1 &= 5\\ x_2 &= -2\\ x_3 &= 7\end{cases}$$

Since the system has a unique solution, the vectors $\boldsymbol{e_1},\boldsymbol{e_2}$, and $\boldsymbol{e_3}$ do form a basis and the coordinates of $\boldsymbol{a}$ in that basis are 5, –2, and 7.

10. Points A and B are given by they coordinates in a Cartesian rectangular system: $A(1, -1, 3)$; $B(7, 8, 12)$. Find the coordinates of such a point M located on the segment AB that $AM : MB = 3:5$.

Solution. Let O be the origin of the coordinate system. We have to find the coordinates of point M that is the coordinates of the position vector $\overrightarrow{OM}$.

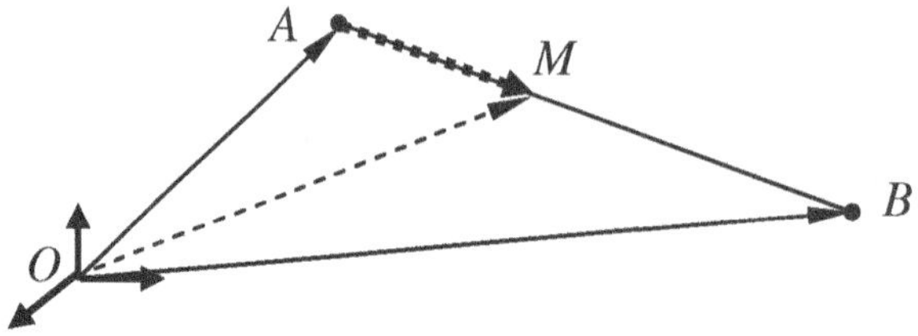

$$\overrightarrow{OM} = \overrightarrow{OA} + \overrightarrow{AM} = \overrightarrow{OA} + \tfrac{3}{3+5}\overrightarrow{AB} = \overrightarrow{OA} + \tfrac{3}{8}\left(\overrightarrow{OB} - \overrightarrow{OA}\right) = \tfrac{5}{8}\overrightarrow{OA} + \tfrac{3}{8}\overrightarrow{OB} = \tfrac{5}{8}\begin{bmatrix}1\\-1\\3\end{bmatrix} + \tfrac{3}{8}\begin{bmatrix}7\\8\\12\end{bmatrix} = \begin{bmatrix}\frac{13}{4}\\\frac{19}{8}\\\frac{51}{8}\end{bmatrix}.$$

Thus, the coordinates of M are $\left(\frac{13}{4}, \frac{19}{8}, \frac{51}{8}\right)$.

2. THE DOT PRODUCT AND CROSS PRODUCT OF VECTORS.

2.1 THE DOT PRODUCT OF VECTORS.

Definition. The dot product of two vectors, ***a*** and ***b***, is defined as the product of the magnitudes (lengths) of these vectors times the cosine of an angle they form:

$$\boldsymbol{a} \cdot \boldsymbol{b} = \|\boldsymbol{a}\| \cdot \|\boldsymbol{b}\| \cos\left(\widehat{\boldsymbol{a}, \boldsymbol{b}}\right). \tag{1}$$

For the sake of brevity, we shall often write

$$\boldsymbol{a} \cdot \boldsymbol{b} = \|\boldsymbol{a}\| \cdot \|\boldsymbol{b}\| \cos\theta, \tag{2}$$

meaning that $\theta = \left(\widehat{\boldsymbol{a}, \boldsymbol{b}}\right)$ is the least of the angles between the vectors, and it is counted in the direction from ***a*** to ***b*** (we shall always count angles from the first vector of the product to the second one, as shown in Figure 1).

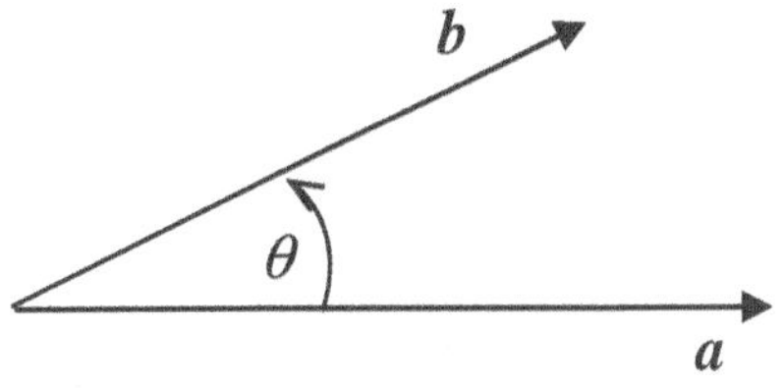

Figure 1

Let us emphasize that the dot product is a *scalar* (number) assigned to a pair of vectors taken in a certain order. That is why it is often called the *scalar product of two vectors*. Also, it is called the *inner product* of vectors.

The dot product emerges naturally in various physical and geometrical problems involving *projections* of vectors onto vectors.

For example, the physical work required to move a body (point mass) along a straight line from one point to another, is defined as the product of the magnitude of the force acting along the line times the length of the displacement:

$$W = \|\boldsymbol{f}\| \cdot \|\boldsymbol{l}\|. \tag{3}$$

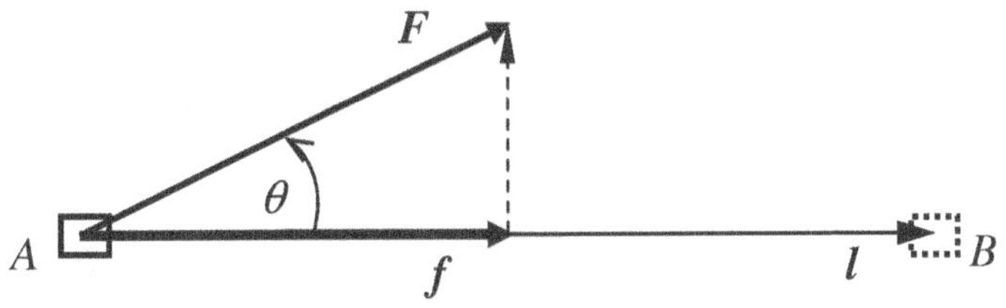

Figure 2

In a more general situation, illustrated in Figure 2, the force ***F***, moving a body from one point *A* to another *B*, is not directed along the displacement $\overrightarrow{AB} = \boldsymbol{l}$; in other words, the vectors ***F*** and ***l*** are not collinear. Then we can present ***F*** as a sum of two *vector components*: one of them, $\boldsymbol{f}$, is collinear with $\boldsymbol{l}$, and it forces the body to move along $\boldsymbol{l}$; the other component is perpendicular to $\boldsymbol{l}$ and therefore it does not produce any effect on the motion in this direction.

The magnitude of the component $\boldsymbol{f}$ can be determined as

$$\|\boldsymbol{F}\|\cos\theta. \tag{4}$$

This magnitude is called *the projection of* **F** *onto the direction of* **l** (for the sake of brevity we shall often omit the words "the direction of").

Vector $\boldsymbol{f}$ itself is also called *the projection*; to avoid confusion we shall use the words *vector projection* for $\boldsymbol{f}$ and *scalar projection* for the expression given by (4). In case it is not specified in the context what kind of projection is considered, we shall suggest the vector projection.

Let us also notice that it follows from the definition of the cosine function that formula (4) holds for any angles, and for obtuse angles the scalar projection is negative. It makes sense from a physical point of view, since if the angle is obtuse the force "works" against the direction of motion.

Now the expression for the physical work can be rewritten as

$$W = (\|\boldsymbol{F}\|\cos\theta)\|\boldsymbol{l}\| = \|\boldsymbol{F}\|\cdot\|\boldsymbol{l}\|\cos\theta = \boldsymbol{F}\cdot\boldsymbol{l}, \tag{5}$$

i.e. it is a dot product of the vectors of force and displacement.

Following the physical analogy, we can define the scalar and vector projections of a vector onto a vector in general. It follows from (2) that

$$\|\boldsymbol{a}\|\cos\theta = \frac{\boldsymbol{a}\cdot\boldsymbol{b}}{\|\boldsymbol{b}\|}, \tag{6}$$

so we can introduce the following definition:

Definition. Given two vectors, $\boldsymbol{a}$ and $\boldsymbol{b}$, the magnitude

$$proj_b\boldsymbol{a} = \frac{\boldsymbol{a}\cdot\boldsymbol{b}}{\|\boldsymbol{b}\|} \tag{7}$$

is called the *scalar projection of* **a** *onto* **b**.

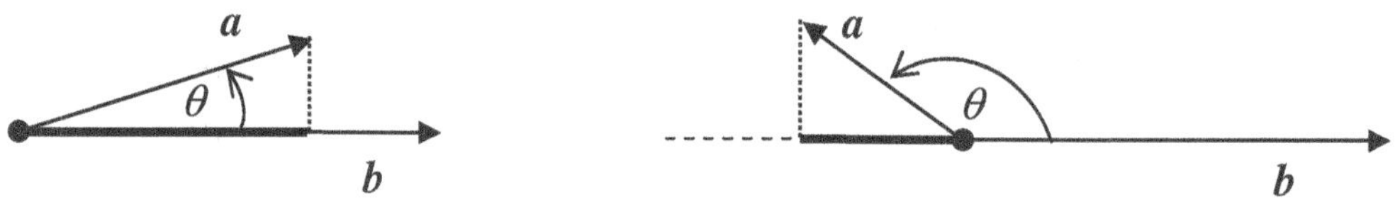

Figure 3

The scalar projection of a vector ($\boldsymbol{a}$) onto a vector ($\boldsymbol{b}$) is *positive* if the vectors form an acute angle and *negative* otherwise, as illustrated in Figure 3. If the vectors are brought to the same origin, one can view the scalar projection as a segment starting at the origin of the vectors and ending at the foot of the perpendicular dropped from the terminal point of $\boldsymbol{a}$ onto the line that contains $\boldsymbol{b}$. Thus the segment is assigned a direction: it is co-directed with $\boldsymbol{b}$ when θ is acute, and the projection is positive in this case, or it is opposite to $\boldsymbol{b}$ when θ is obtuse, which implies a negative projection.

The *vector projection* joins the same two points as the segment representing the scalar projection: its origin coincides with the origin of the segment, and its terminal point lies at the terminal point of the segment. Thus the vector projection is a vector collinear with vector $\boldsymbol{b}$, on which we project. It is co-directed with $\boldsymbol{b}$ when the vectors $\boldsymbol{a}$ and $\boldsymbol{b}$ form an acute angle and oppositely directed otherwise (Figure 4).

In order to make a vector out of a scalar, we shall multiply the scalar by a *unit vector* (a vector of length 1) in the direction of vector $\boldsymbol{b}$. It is easy to verify that such a unit vector is

$$\boldsymbol{u} = \frac{1}{\|\boldsymbol{b}\|}\boldsymbol{b}. \tag{8}$$

Really, according to the definition of multiplication of vectors by numbers, vector $\boldsymbol{u}$ will have the same direction as $\boldsymbol{b}$ and its norm will be 1:

$$\|\boldsymbol{u}\| = \left|\frac{1}{\|\boldsymbol{b}\|}\right| \cdot \|\boldsymbol{b}\| = \frac{1}{\|\boldsymbol{b}\|}\|\boldsymbol{b}\| = 1. \tag{9}$$

Definition. Given two vectors, $\boldsymbol{a}$ and $\boldsymbol{b}$, with an angle θ between them, the vector

$$\overrightarrow{proj_b \boldsymbol{a}} = \left(\frac{\boldsymbol{a}\cdot\boldsymbol{b}}{\|\boldsymbol{b}\|}\right)\frac{1}{\|\boldsymbol{b}\|}\boldsymbol{b} = \frac{\boldsymbol{a}\cdot\boldsymbol{b}}{\|\boldsymbol{b}\|^2}\boldsymbol{b} \tag{10}$$

is called the vector projection of $\boldsymbol{a}$ onto $\boldsymbol{b}$.

In some texts they say *orthogonal projection* instead of *projection.* As we shall see soon, the word *orthogonal* is a synonym of *perpendicular.*

Figure 4

The dot product possesses the following properties:

Theorem 2.1.1 For any vectors $\boldsymbol{a}$ and $\boldsymbol{b}$,
(i) $\boldsymbol{a}\cdot\boldsymbol{b} = \boldsymbol{b}\cdot\boldsymbol{a}$
(ii) $\boldsymbol{a}\cdot(\boldsymbol{b}+\boldsymbol{c}) = \boldsymbol{a}\cdot\boldsymbol{b} + \boldsymbol{a}\cdot\boldsymbol{c}$
(iii) $(k\boldsymbol{a})\cdot\boldsymbol{b} = k(\boldsymbol{a}\cdot\boldsymbol{b})$ for any number k
(iv) $\boldsymbol{a}\cdot\boldsymbol{a} \geq 0$, and the equality holds if and only if $\boldsymbol{a} = \boldsymbol{0}$.

Proof. The proofs are really easy. Hint: when proving (ii), use projections onto $\boldsymbol{a}$.

Orthogonal vectors.

If two vectors are perpendicular to each other, the cosine of the angle between them is equal to 0.

If one of these vectors is a zero-vector, then its magnitude is 0. In either case their dot product is zero:

$$a \cdot b = 0 \tag{11}$$

Formula (11) is called the *orthogonality condition.*

Definition. Two vectors are said to be *orthogonal* if their dot product is equal to 0.

One can easily show that if two vectors are orthogonal, i.e. (11) is satisfied, then either they are mutually perpendicular or at least one of them is a zero vector. (As the direction of a zero vector is undefined, one can say that they are perpendicular in either of these cases). Thus we have the following result.

Theorem 2.1.2 Two vectors are orthogonal if and only if they are perpendicular.

The magnitude (norm) of a vector.

According to the definition, the dot product of a vector by itself equals its length squared (why?):

$$v \cdot v = \|v\|^2 \tag{12}$$

From this equality, one can use the properties of the dot product to find the magnitude of a vector. In particular, it is often used to find a *unit vector* – a vector of magnitude 1 in a given direction (see Example 1 below).

The coordinate representation of the dot product.

A basis in the space of geometric vectors is formed by three noncoplanar vectors taken in a certain order. If these vectors are mutually orthogonal, we shall call such a basis *orthogonal.* If they are orthogonal and each of them is a unit vector, we call such a basis *orthonormal.*

The vectors of an orthonormal basis are usually denoted $\boldsymbol{i}, \boldsymbol{j}$, and $\boldsymbol{k}$. The conditions for $\{\boldsymbol{i}, \boldsymbol{j}, \boldsymbol{k}\}$ to be an orthonormal basis can be written as

$$\boldsymbol{i} \cdot \boldsymbol{j} = \boldsymbol{j} \cdot \boldsymbol{k} = \boldsymbol{k} \cdot \boldsymbol{i} = 0; \tag{13}$$

$$\|\boldsymbol{i}\| = \|\boldsymbol{j}\| = \|\boldsymbol{k}\| = 1. \tag{14}$$

If a Cartesian coordinate system is built upon such a basis, the corresponding axes are denoted the *Ox*, *Oy*, and *Oz* (or just *X*, *Y*, and *Z*) –axes respectively (Figure 5).

Such a coordinate system is called a *rectangular Cartesian coordinate system.* We shall suggest that such a system is being used and that the $\{\boldsymbol{i}, \boldsymbol{j}, \boldsymbol{k}\}$-basis is in correspondence with the standard basis in R^3, unless specified otherwise, i.e. we shall identify:

$$i = \begin{bmatrix} 1 \\ 0 \\ 0 \end{bmatrix}; \quad j = \begin{bmatrix} 0 \\ 1 \\ 0 \end{bmatrix}; \quad k = \begin{bmatrix} 0 \\ 0 \\ 1 \end{bmatrix}. \tag{15}$$

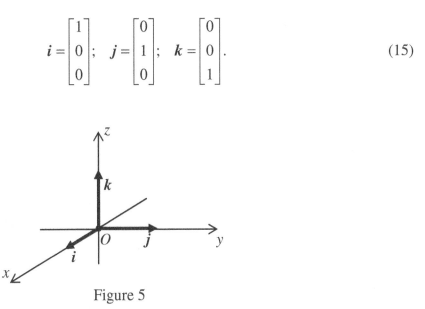

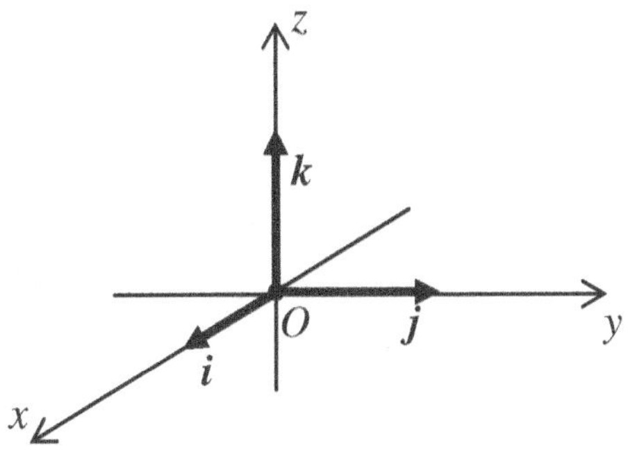

Figure 5

An orthonormal basis is convenient since the dot product of two vectors given by their components in such a basis is described by a simple formula. Let us derive it.

Theorem 2.1.3 Let $\boldsymbol{u}$ and $\boldsymbol{v}$ be two vectors given by their expansions in an orthonormal basis

$$\boldsymbol{u} = u_1\boldsymbol{i} + u_2\boldsymbol{j} + u_3\boldsymbol{k}; \quad \boldsymbol{v} = v_1\boldsymbol{i} + v_2\boldsymbol{j} + v_3\boldsymbol{k}. \tag{16}$$

Then their dot product is

$$\boxed{\boldsymbol{u}\cdot\boldsymbol{v} = u_1v_1 + u_2v_2 + u_3v_3}. \tag{17}$$

Proof. Hint: use the properties of dot products and conditions (13) and (14).

Following this result, one can determine the magnitude of any vector $\boldsymbol{a}$ if its coordinates (a_1, a_2, a_3) in an orthonormal basis are known:

$$\|\boldsymbol{a}\| = \sqrt{a_1^2 + a_2^2 + a_3^2} \tag{18}$$

Example 1. Find a unit vector in the direction of vector $\boldsymbol{a}$= (-2, 1, 2).
Solution. As we have already shown in the beginning of the section, the required vector can be found as

$$\boldsymbol{u} = \frac{1}{\|\boldsymbol{a}\|}\boldsymbol{a}. \tag{19}$$

Then,

$$\boldsymbol{u} = \frac{1}{\sqrt{(-2)^2 + 1^2 + 2^2}}(-2, 1, 2) = (-\tfrac{2}{3}, \tfrac{1}{3}, \tfrac{2}{3}). \ \square$$

The *distance between two points* given by their Cartesian coordinates can be determined as the length of a vector joining these points. For points $A(x_A, y_A, z_A)$ and $B(x_B, y_B, z_B)$ it will be

$$dist(A,B) = \left\|\overrightarrow{AB}\right\| = \sqrt{(x_B - x_A)^2 + (y_B - y_A)^2 + (z_B - z_A)^2} \quad (20)$$

Applications of dot products.

The dot product of vectors is often used for solving geometrical problems involving projections, lengths, angles, and orthogonality.

2. 2 THE CROSS PRODUCT OF VECTORS

Definition. The cross product of two vectors, ***a*** and ***b***, is such a vector $\boldsymbol{c} = \boldsymbol{a} \times \boldsymbol{b}$ that:

(1) $\|\boldsymbol{c}\| = \|\boldsymbol{a}\| \cdot \|\boldsymbol{b}\| \sin\theta$ = the numerical expression of the area of a parallelogram constructed on ***a*** and ***b*** (Figure 4);

(2) ***c*** is orthogonal to ***a*** and to ***b***;

(3) ***a***, ***b***, and ***c*** form a right triple of vectors, i.e. from the endpoint of ***c***, the shortest rotation from ***a*** to ***b*** is seen counter-clockwise.

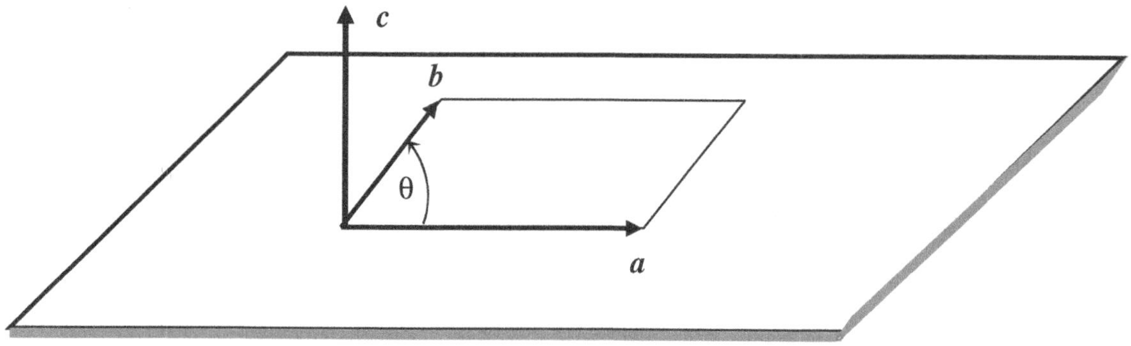

Figure 1

It follows from the definition that the magnitude (norm) of the cross product of two vectors is *numerically equal to the area of a parallelogram* constructed on these vectors: $Area(\square) = \|\boldsymbol{a}\| \cdot h = \|\boldsymbol{a}\| \cdot \|\boldsymbol{b}\| \sin\theta$, as one can see from Figure 2.

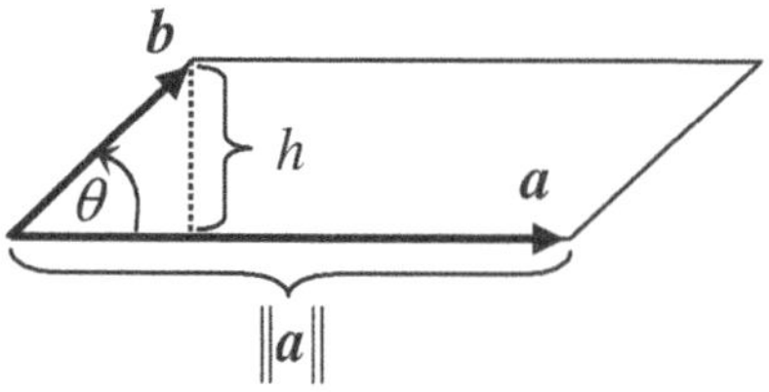

Figure 2

The cross product is a vector; that is why it is often called the *vector product of vectors*. Also, it is called the *outer product*.

Physical interpretations of the cross product.

Numerous physical characteristics such as the angular momentum, angular velocity, torque, Lorentz force (the force acting on a charge moving in a magnetic field), are introduced as cross products.

For example, let us consider a particle of mass m moving with varying velocity $\boldsymbol{v}$ along some curve in a plane (P). Point A will denote the position of the particle at each given instance. Its linear momentum (which in common language can be characterized as "the amount of motion") is, by definition, the vector $m\boldsymbol{v}$. Let us explain why the *angular momentum* of such a particle about some other point O of this plane, is defined as the cross product of the position vector $\overrightarrow{OA} = \boldsymbol{r}$ of point A with respect to O by the linear momentum $m\boldsymbol{v}$: $\boldsymbol{L} = \boldsymbol{r} \times m\boldsymbol{v}$.

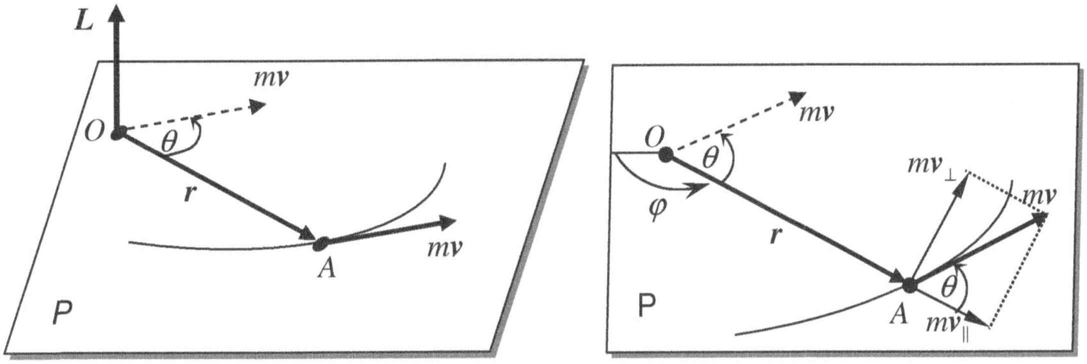

(a) Figure 3 (b)

The diagrams in Figure 3 explain why such a definition emerges. Both diagrams in this figure illustrate the same situation. In Figure 3a we see the space picture, whereas Figure 3b shows the view of the plane as it is seen by someone looking straight down at the plane (for instance, we cannot see vector $\boldsymbol{L}$ in Figure 3b since it is directed right towards the spectators and therefore projects itself into one point).

Since the particle moves in plane P, we can fix the direction of $\boldsymbol{L}$ by choosing it to be perpendicular to the plane. The axis about which the particle rotates would likewise be perpendicular. (The conservation law for the angular momentum implies that the direction of the plane, in which rotation occurs, does not change). Then we can choose whether $\boldsymbol{L}$ is directed "upward" or "downward". This is a mere convention, and we shall choose the "upward" direction, according to the so-called *right hand rule*, i.e. we require that the vectors $\boldsymbol{r}$, $m\boldsymbol{v}$, and $\boldsymbol{L}$ form a *right triple* (Figure 3a). Thus the direction of $\boldsymbol{L}$ has been determined, and it coincides with the direction of $\boldsymbol{r} \times m\boldsymbol{v}$.

As for the magnitude of the angular momentum, it should show the "amount of motion" of the rotational motion in the plane. Let us show that this magnitude is really determined by the expression $\|\boldsymbol{r}\| \cdot \|m\boldsymbol{v}\| \sin\theta$, which is the norm of the cross product $\boldsymbol{r} \times m\boldsymbol{v}$. It is natural that the magnitude of the angular momentum is proportional to the radius of revolution, which is $\boldsymbol{r}$, and to the magnitude of the momentum of motion around O. The momentum vector $m\boldsymbol{v}$ can be decomposed into a sum of two components, as shown in Figure 3b:

$$mv = mv_{\|} + mv_{\perp} . \tag{21}$$

One of the components, denoted $mv_{\|}$, is collinear with the position vector, and hence it characterizes the motion towards or from but not around point O. The other component, $mv_{\perp}$, is perpendicular to the position vector, and hence this is the component that determines the momentum of the circular motion about O. The magnitude of these components, as we can see from the diagram, is

$$mv_{\perp} = \|mv\| \sin\theta . \tag{22}$$

Therefore, the magnitude of the angular momentum can be determined as

$$\|\boldsymbol{r}\| \cdot \|mv_{\perp}\| = \|\boldsymbol{r}\| \|mv\| \sin\theta , \tag{23}$$

which is the magnitude of the cross product $\boldsymbol{r} \times mv$.

To summarize this brief discussion, one can say that in some sense we had to define the angular momentum as a cross product.

Similarly, this notion emerges naturally when considering the motion of charged particles in magnetic fields. Experiments have shown that when charged particles enter a magnetic field, they deflect from a straight trajectory and start moving along a circle or along a helix. This can be interpreted as the existence of a force perpendicular to the vector of magnetic field and to the component of the velocity that is perpendicular to the field. Therefore this force, called the Lorentz force, has been defined as a force proportional to the cross product of the vectors of velocity $\boldsymbol{v}$ and magnetic field $\boldsymbol{B}$:

$$\boldsymbol{F}_L = q\boldsymbol{v} \times \boldsymbol{B} . \tag{24}$$

In this formula, q is a scalar (some physical constant depending on physical units).

Thus the notion of cross product, unusual as it appears in the beginning, emerges naturally in physics.

The properties of cross products.

The properties of the cross product are stated in the next theorem:

Theorem 2.2.1 For any vectors $\boldsymbol{a}$ and $\boldsymbol{b}$,

(i) $\boldsymbol{a} \times \boldsymbol{b} = -\boldsymbol{b} \times \boldsymbol{a}$

(ii) $\boldsymbol{a} \times (\boldsymbol{b} + \boldsymbol{c}) = \boldsymbol{a} \times \boldsymbol{b} + \boldsymbol{a} \times \boldsymbol{c}$

(iii) $(k\boldsymbol{a}) \times \boldsymbol{b} = k(\boldsymbol{a} \times \boldsymbol{b})$ for any number k

(iv) $\boldsymbol{a} \times \boldsymbol{a} = \boldsymbol{0}$

Proof. The proof is omitted (it is easy to prove all of these except, maybe, (ii)).

These properties can be used to derive the expression of the cross product of vectors given by their components. The expression can be represented in a convenient symbolic form by means of the so-called *determinants*.

Determinants of order 2 and 3.

A rectangular array of numbers or symbols consisting of m rows and n columns is called an $m\times n$ matrix. In this section we shall be interested in such matrices, for which the number of rows and columns is the same; they are called square matrices. For example,

$$A=\begin{bmatrix} a & b \\ c & d \end{bmatrix} \tag{1}$$

is a square (2×2) matrix, and

$$A=\begin{bmatrix} x & y & z \\ a & b & c \\ \alpha & \beta & \gamma \end{bmatrix} \tag{2}$$

is a square 3×3 matrix.

It is convenient to number each entry of a matrix by two subscripts: first of them is the number of the row and second – the number of the column in which the entry is located. For example, for A given by (2), $x=a_{11}$; $y=a_{12}$; $z=a_{13}$; $a=a_{21}$;... $\gamma=a_{33}$, and thus we can present a general 3×3 matrix as

$$A=\begin{bmatrix} a_{11} & a_{12} & a_{13} \\ a_{21} & a_{22} & a_{23} \\ a_{31} & a_{32} & a_{33} \end{bmatrix} \tag{3}$$

Each square matrix is assigned a quantity, which is calculated as a certain combination of the entries of the matrix. This quantity is called the *determinant* of the matrix. It is an important algebraic characteristic of a matrix, which also possesses some geometrical meaning. In this section, we shall consider only the determinants of 2×2 and 3×3 matrices, which are called the determinants of order 2 and 3 respectively.

Definition. The determinant of a 1×1 matrix is, by definition, equal to the only entry of the matrix.

Definition. The determinant of a 2×2 matrix $A=\begin{bmatrix} a & b \\ c & d \end{bmatrix}$ is

$$\det A=\det\begin{bmatrix} a & b \\ c & d \end{bmatrix}=\begin{vmatrix} a & b \\ c & d \end{vmatrix}=ad-bc. \tag{4}$$

Example 1. $\det\begin{bmatrix} 2 & 4 \\ -1 & 3 \end{bmatrix}=\begin{vmatrix} 2 & 4 \\ -1 & 3 \end{vmatrix}=2\cdot 3-4\cdot(-1)=10.$

Definition. The determinant of a matrix obtained from a given matrix by eliminating all the entries of the row number i and column number j is called the ij –th *minor* (or the minor associated with entry a_{ij}) and it is denoted M_{ij}.

Definition. The number $C_{ij} = (-1)^{i+j} M_{ij}$ is called the *cofactor of entry* a_{ij}.

It follows from the last definition that a cofactor C_{ij} is equal to the corresponding minor M_{ij} if $i + j$ is even or to the negative of the corresponding minor if $i + j$ is odd.

Example 2. For matrix $A = \begin{bmatrix} a & b \\ c & d \end{bmatrix}$,

$$M_{11} = d;\quad C_{11} = (-1)^{1+1} M_{11} = d;\quad M_{12} = c;\quad C_{12} = (-1)^{1+2} M_{12} = -M_{12} = -c.$$

Example 3. For matrix $B = \begin{bmatrix} -3 & -9 \\ 2 & 5 \end{bmatrix}$,

$$M_{11} = 5;\quad C_{11} = (-1)^{1+1} M_{11} = 5;\quad M_{12} = 2;\quad C_{12} = (-1)^{1+2} M_{12} = -M_{12} = -2;$$
$$M_{21} = -9;\quad C_{21} = (-1)^{2+1} M_{21} = 9;\quad M_{22} = -3;\quad C_{22} = (-1)^{2+2} M_{22} = M_{22} = -3.$$

Example 4. For matrix A given by formula (2), we can find M_{32} by evaluating the determinant of the 2×2 matrix consisting of all the entries of A that are left after all the entries of the 3rd row and 2nd column have been eliminated as shown in the diagram below.

$$A = \begin{bmatrix} x & \cancel{y} & z \\ a & \cancel{b} & c \\ \cancel{\alpha} & \cancel{\beta} & \cancel{\gamma} \end{bmatrix};\ M_{32} = \det \begin{bmatrix} x & z \\ a & c \end{bmatrix} = xc - za;\ C_{32} = (-1)^{3+2} M_{32} = -M_{32} = -xc + za.$$

Similarly, one can find: $C_{11} = (-1)^{1+1} M_{11} = (-1)^2 M_{11} = M_{11} = \begin{vmatrix} b & c \\ \beta & \gamma \end{vmatrix} = b\gamma - c\beta;$

$$C_{12} = (-1)^{1+2} M_{12} = -M_{12} = -\begin{vmatrix} a & c \\ \alpha & \gamma \end{vmatrix} = -(a\gamma - c\alpha) = c\alpha - a\gamma;$$

$$C_{23} = (-1)^{2+3} M_{23} = -M_{23} = -\begin{vmatrix} x & y \\ \alpha & \beta \end{vmatrix} = -x\beta + y\alpha.$$

Example 5. For matrix $M = \begin{bmatrix} 2 & 1 & 0 \\ -1 & 3 & 2 \\ -2 & 1 & 0 \end{bmatrix}$,

$$C_{11} = (-1)^{1+1} M_{11} = M_{11} = \begin{vmatrix} 3 & 2 \\ 1 & 0 \end{vmatrix} = -2;\quad C_{23} = -M_{23} = -\begin{bmatrix} 2 & 1 \\ -2 & 1 \end{bmatrix} = -(2+2) = -4.$$

Definition. The determinant of a 3×3 matrix is equal to the sum of the products of all entries of the first row of the matrix by the corresponding cofactors:

$$\det\begin{bmatrix} a_{11} & a_{12} & a_{13} \\ a_{21} & a_{22} & a_{23} \\ a_{31} & a_{32} & a_{33} \end{bmatrix} = \begin{vmatrix} a_{11} & a_{12} & a_{13} \\ a_{21} & a_{22} & a_{23} \\ a_{31} & a_{32} & a_{33} \end{vmatrix} = a_{11}C_{11} + a_{12}C_{12} + a_{13}C_{13} \qquad (5)$$

This definition presents the determinant by means of an *expansion along the first row*.

Example 6. Let us evaluate the determinant of matrix M from Example 5.

$$\det M = \begin{vmatrix} 2 & 1 & 0 \\ -1 & 3 & 2 \\ -2 & 1 & 0 \end{vmatrix} = 2(-1)^{1+1}\begin{vmatrix} 3 & 2 \\ 1 & 0 \end{vmatrix} + 1(-1)^{1+2}\begin{vmatrix} -1 & 2 \\ -2 & 0 \end{vmatrix} + 0(-1)^{1+3}\begin{vmatrix} -1 & 3 \\ -2 & 1 \end{vmatrix} = -8.$$

It can be proved that the determinant of a matrix can be evaluated by means of a similar expansion along any row or column, and a more general definition of the determinant can be given. However, for the tasks of this section, the above definition is sufficient.

The coordinate representation of cross products.

Theorem 2.2.2 Let $\boldsymbol{u}$ and $\boldsymbol{v}$ be two vectors given by their expansions in an orthonormal basis: $\boldsymbol{u} = u_1\boldsymbol{i} + u_2\boldsymbol{j} + u_3\boldsymbol{k}$; $\boldsymbol{v} = v_1\boldsymbol{i} + v_2\boldsymbol{j} + v_3\boldsymbol{k}$.

Then their cross product can be presented in symbolic form as

$$\boldsymbol{u}\times\boldsymbol{v} = \begin{vmatrix} \boldsymbol{i} & \boldsymbol{j} & \boldsymbol{k} \\ u_1 & u_2 & u_3 \\ v_1 & v_2 & v_3 \end{vmatrix} \qquad (6)$$

Proof. First, let us evaluate the cross products of all possible pairs of vectors that constitute an orthonormal basis.

According to property (iv),

$$\boldsymbol{i}\times\boldsymbol{i} = \boldsymbol{j}\times\boldsymbol{j} = \boldsymbol{k}\times\boldsymbol{k} = \boldsymbol{0}. \qquad (7)$$

It follows from the definition that $\boldsymbol{i}\times\boldsymbol{j}$ is a unit vector perpendicular to the plane of the vectors $\boldsymbol{i}$ and $\boldsymbol{j}$, and making a right triple with them. Therefore, it is $\boldsymbol{k}$. Similarly, one can find all the following products:

$$\boldsymbol{i}\times\boldsymbol{j} = \boldsymbol{k}; \boldsymbol{j}\times\boldsymbol{i} = -\boldsymbol{k}; \quad \boldsymbol{j}\times\boldsymbol{k} = \boldsymbol{i}; \boldsymbol{k}\times\boldsymbol{j} = -\boldsymbol{i}; \quad \boldsymbol{k}\times\boldsymbol{i} = \boldsymbol{j}; \boldsymbol{i}\times\boldsymbol{k} = -\boldsymbol{j}. \qquad (8)$$

Now we can take these identities into account and carry out the calculations:

$$
\begin{aligned}
\boldsymbol{u}\times\boldsymbol{v} &= (u_1\boldsymbol{i}+u_2\boldsymbol{j}+u_3\boldsymbol{k})\times(v_1\boldsymbol{i}+v_2\boldsymbol{j}+v_3\boldsymbol{k}) = \\
&= (u_1v_2-u_2v_1)\boldsymbol{i}\times\boldsymbol{j}+(u_1v_3-u_3v_1)\boldsymbol{i}\times\boldsymbol{k}+(u_3v_2-u_2v_3)\boldsymbol{k}\times\boldsymbol{j} = \\
&= (u_1v_2-u_2v_1)\boldsymbol{k}-(u_1v_3-u_3v_1)\boldsymbol{j}+(u_2v_3-u_3v_2)\boldsymbol{i} = \\
&= \begin{vmatrix} u_2 & u_3 \\ v_2 & v_3 \end{vmatrix}\boldsymbol{i}-\begin{vmatrix} u_1 & u_3 \\ v_1 & v_3 \end{vmatrix}\boldsymbol{j}+\begin{vmatrix} u_1 & u_2 \\ v_1 & v_2 \end{vmatrix}\boldsymbol{k}.
\end{aligned}
\tag{9}
$$

The latter expression can be viewed as the expansion of the determinant from (6) along the first row. □

Applications of cross products. Geometrical meaning of determinants.

Cross product has two basic applications in Analytic Geometry (geometry via formulae): 1) to compute areas of rectilinear figures (parallelograms, triangles, etc.);
2) to construct vectors perpendicular to given two vectors, and therefore perpendicular to planes..

Example 7. Evaluate the area of a parallelogram constructed upon two vectors lying in the *XOY*-plane:

$$\boldsymbol{u}=u_1\boldsymbol{i}+u_2\boldsymbol{j};\quad \boldsymbol{v}=v_1\boldsymbol{i}+v_2\boldsymbol{j}. \tag{10}$$

Solution. According to the definition,

$$Area(\square)=\|\boldsymbol{u}\times\boldsymbol{v}\|. \tag{11}$$

We shall use the expression (6) to evaluate the cross product:

$$\boldsymbol{u}\times\boldsymbol{v}=\begin{vmatrix} \boldsymbol{i} & \boldsymbol{j} & \boldsymbol{k} \\ u_1 & u_2 & 0 \\ v_1 & v_2 & 0 \end{vmatrix}=0\cdot\boldsymbol{i}+0\cdot\boldsymbol{j}+\begin{vmatrix} u_1 & u_2 \\ v_1 & v_2 \end{vmatrix}\boldsymbol{k}=\left(\det\begin{bmatrix} u_1 & u_2 \\ v_1 & v_2 \end{bmatrix}\right)\boldsymbol{k}. \tag{12}$$

Then we obtain for the area:

$$Area(\square)=\left\|\left(\det\begin{bmatrix} u_1 & u_2 \\ v_1 & v_2 \end{bmatrix}\right)\boldsymbol{k}\right\|=\left|\det\begin{bmatrix} u_1 & u_2 \\ v_1 & v_2 \end{bmatrix}\right|\cdot\|\boldsymbol{k}\|=\left|\det\begin{bmatrix} u_1 & u_2 \\ v_1 & v_2 \end{bmatrix}\right|. \tag{13}$$

Thus the absolute value of the determinant composed of the coordinates of two vectors equals to the area of a parallelogram constructed on these vectors! This is quite amazing, since the definition of the determinant seems to be "very abstract'.

Later on we will show that a similar interpretation exists for the third order determinants: the absolute value of a 3×3 determinant whose rows are the coordinates of vectors, is equal to the volume of a parallelepiped constructed upon these vectors.

The triple product of vectors.

Definition. Let ***a***, ***b***, and ***c*** be three vectors. The scalar

$$\boldsymbol{a}\cdot(\boldsymbol{b}\times\boldsymbol{c}) \tag{14}$$

is called the triple product of these vectors.

The triple product is also called the *scalar triple* or the *mixed* product of vectors. Its properties and geometrical meaning are determined by those of the dot and cross products.

We shall start with the geometrical interpretation of the triple product.

Let us consider three vectors $\boldsymbol{a}$, $\boldsymbol{b}$, and $\boldsymbol{c}$ that form a right triple of vectors: the shortest rotation from $\boldsymbol{b}$ to $\boldsymbol{c}$ is seen from the terminal point of $\boldsymbol{a}$ in the counterclockwise direction. In this case, the angle between $\boldsymbol{a}$ and $\boldsymbol{b}\times\boldsymbol{c}$ is acute, and the scalar projection of $\boldsymbol{a}$ onto the direction of $\boldsymbol{b}\times\boldsymbol{c}$ is positive. As one can see from Figure 4, this projection is equal to the altitude H of the parallelepiped constructed on $\boldsymbol{a}$, $\boldsymbol{b}$, and $\boldsymbol{c}$.

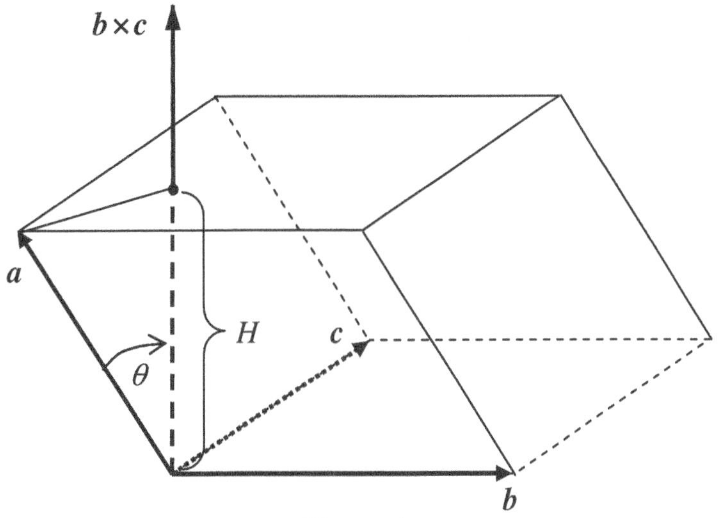

Figure 4

According to the definitions of the dot and cross products,

$$\boldsymbol{a}\cdot(\boldsymbol{b}\times\boldsymbol{c}) = \|\boldsymbol{a}\|\cdot\|\boldsymbol{b}\times\boldsymbol{c}\|\cos\theta = \left(\|\boldsymbol{a}\|\cos\theta\right)\cdot\|\boldsymbol{b}\times\boldsymbol{c}\| = H\cdot Area(\square) = V\,, \tag{15}$$

where V is the volume of the parallelepiped constructed on $\boldsymbol{a}$, $\boldsymbol{b}$, and $\boldsymbol{c}$.

In case when $\boldsymbol{a}$, $\boldsymbol{b}$, and $\boldsymbol{c}$ form a left triple, the angle θ between $\boldsymbol{a}$ and $\boldsymbol{b}\times\boldsymbol{c}$ will be obtuse; then we shall have $H=-\|\boldsymbol{a}\|\cos\theta$, and respectively

$$\boldsymbol{a}\cdot(\boldsymbol{b}\times\boldsymbol{c}) = \|\boldsymbol{a}\|\cdot\|\boldsymbol{b}\times\boldsymbol{c}\|\cos\theta = \left(\|\boldsymbol{a}\|\cos\theta\right)\cdot\|\boldsymbol{b}\times\boldsymbol{c}\| = -H\cdot Area(\square) = -V\,. \tag{16}$$

Thus we have established the following important result:

<u>Theorem 2.2.3</u> The triple product of three noncoplanar vectors is equal to the volume of the parallelepiped constructed on these vectors if they form a right triple and it is equal to the negative of that volume if they form a left triple:

$$\begin{cases} \boldsymbol{a}\cdot(\boldsymbol{b}\times\boldsymbol{c}) = V & \text{if } \boldsymbol{a},\boldsymbol{b},\boldsymbol{c} \text{ is a right triple;} \\ \boldsymbol{a}\cdot(\boldsymbol{b}\times\boldsymbol{c}) = -V & \text{if } \boldsymbol{a},\boldsymbol{b},\boldsymbol{c} \text{ is a left triple.} \end{cases} \tag{17}$$

This result is used in two kinds of problems:

(i) for evaluating volumes;

(ii) for determining if three given vectors form a right or a left triple.

Theorem 2.2.4 If three vectors are coplanar, their triple product is equal to 0.

Proof. If $\boldsymbol{a}$, $\boldsymbol{b}$, and $\boldsymbol{c}$ are coplanar, then $\boldsymbol{b}\times\boldsymbol{c}$ will be orthogonal to $\boldsymbol{a}$, hence their dot product will be equal to 0. □

The following theorems follow immediately from the above results, and properties of the dot and cross products, and their proofs are left for students.

Theorem 2.2.5

$$\boldsymbol{a}\cdot(\boldsymbol{b}\times\boldsymbol{c}) = (\boldsymbol{a}\times\boldsymbol{b})\cdot\boldsymbol{c} \tag{18}$$

Thanks to this result we shall often denote the triple product $(\boldsymbol{abc})$, without specifying which of the vectors participate in the cross product.

Theorem 2.2.6 The triple product does not change as a result of a cyclical permutation, and

$$(\boldsymbol{abc}) = (\boldsymbol{cab}) = (\boldsymbol{bca}) = -(\boldsymbol{bac}) = -(\boldsymbol{cba}) = -(\boldsymbol{acb})\,. \tag{19}$$

Theorem 2.2.7 The triple product of $\boldsymbol{a}$, $\boldsymbol{b}$, and $\boldsymbol{c}$ given by their coordinates in an orthonormal basis

$$\boldsymbol{a} = a_1\boldsymbol{i} + a_2\boldsymbol{j} + a_3\boldsymbol{k};\quad \boldsymbol{b} = b_1\boldsymbol{i} + b_2\boldsymbol{j} + b_3\boldsymbol{k};\quad \boldsymbol{c} = c_1\boldsymbol{i} + c_2\boldsymbol{j} + c_3\boldsymbol{k}\,, \tag{20}$$

is equal to the determinant of a matrix whose entries are the components of these vectors:

$$(\boldsymbol{abc}) = \begin{vmatrix} a_1 & a_2 & a_3 \\ b_1 & b_2 & b_3 \\ c_1 & c_2 & c_3 \end{vmatrix}. \tag{21}$$

Thus we have discover the geometrical meaning of third order determinants: the absolute value of such a determinant is a volume of a parallelepiped in 3-space.

PRACTICE PROBLEMS (Section 2: The Dot and Cross products of Vectors)

1. It is known that $\|\boldsymbol{a}\| = 1; \|\boldsymbol{b}\| = 2$. Find all the values of t, for which vectors $3\boldsymbol{a} + t\boldsymbol{b}$ and $3\boldsymbol{a} - t\boldsymbol{b}$ are orthogonal.

2. It is given: $\|\boldsymbol{m}\| = 4;\ \|\boldsymbol{n}\| = \sqrt{2};\ (\boldsymbol{m}\hat{,}\boldsymbol{n}) = 135^0$. Find the norm of the vector $\boldsymbol{m} + 3\boldsymbol{n}$.

3. $\boldsymbol{a}$, $\boldsymbol{b}$, and $\boldsymbol{c}$ are three unit vectors satisfying the condition $\boldsymbol{a} + \boldsymbol{b} + \boldsymbol{c} = \boldsymbol{0}$. Evaluate $\boldsymbol{a} \cdot \boldsymbol{b} + \boldsymbol{b} \cdot \boldsymbol{c} + \boldsymbol{c} \cdot \boldsymbol{a}$.

4. Vectors $\boldsymbol{a}$ and $\boldsymbol{b}$ are given by their coordinates in the standard basis $\{\boldsymbol{i}, \boldsymbol{j}, \boldsymbol{k}\}$: $\boldsymbol{a} = (1, -2, 2)$; $\boldsymbol{b} = (1, 0, 1)$. Find: (i) the orthogonal projection of $\boldsymbol{a}$ onto $\boldsymbol{a} - 2\boldsymbol{b}$; (ii) an angle between $\boldsymbol{a}$ and $\boldsymbol{a} + \boldsymbol{b}$.

5. Evaluate the area of a parallelogram formed by vectors $3\boldsymbol{a} + \boldsymbol{b}$ and $\boldsymbol{a} - \boldsymbol{b}$, if $\|\boldsymbol{a}\| = 1;\ \|\boldsymbol{b}\| = 3;\ (\boldsymbol{a}\hat{,}\boldsymbol{b}) = 30^0$.

6. Vectors $\boldsymbol{a}$ and $\boldsymbol{b}$ are given by their coordinates in the standard basis $\{\boldsymbol{i}, \boldsymbol{j}, \boldsymbol{k}\}$: $\boldsymbol{a} = (2, -1, 1)$; $\boldsymbol{b} = (1, 0, -1)$. Find the unit vector perpendicular to both vectors $\boldsymbol{a}$ and $\boldsymbol{b}$ and forming an obtuse angle with the positive Y-semi-axis.

7. Four points are given by their coordinates: $A(1, 0, 2)$; $B(0, 1, 3)$; $C(1, 1, -1)$; and $D(1, 1, 4)$.

   (i) Evaluate the area of triangle BCD;

   (ii) Determine, if these four points are lying in one plane;

   (iii) Evaluate the volume of the pyramid $ABCD$.

SOLUTIONS TO PRACTICE PROBLEMS (Section 2)

1. It is known that $\|\boldsymbol{a}\| = 1; \|\boldsymbol{b}\| = 2.$ Find all the values of t, for which vectors $3\boldsymbol{a} + t\boldsymbol{b}$ and $3\boldsymbol{a} - t\boldsymbol{b}$ are orthogonal.

Solution.

Let us write the orthogonality condition for the vectors $3\boldsymbol{a} + t\boldsymbol{b}$ and $3\boldsymbol{a} - t\boldsymbol{b}$:

$$(3\boldsymbol{a}+t\boldsymbol{b})\cdot(3\boldsymbol{a}-t\boldsymbol{b})=0; \;\Rightarrow\; 9\boldsymbol{a}\cdot\boldsymbol{a}-(3\boldsymbol{a})\cdot(t\boldsymbol{b})+(t\boldsymbol{b})\cdot(3\boldsymbol{a})-(t\boldsymbol{b})\cdot(t\boldsymbol{b})=0;\Rightarrow$$
$$9\|\boldsymbol{a}\|^2-3t\boldsymbol{a}\cdot\boldsymbol{b}+3t\boldsymbol{b}\cdot\boldsymbol{a}-t^2\|\boldsymbol{b}\|^2=0; \;\Rightarrow\; 9\|\boldsymbol{a}\|^2-t^2\|\boldsymbol{b}\|^2=0 \;\Rightarrow\; 9\|\boldsymbol{a}\|^2=t^2\|\boldsymbol{b}\|^2;$$
$$\Rightarrow\; t=\pm\frac{3\|\boldsymbol{a}\|}{\|\boldsymbol{b}\|}=\pm\frac{3}{2}.$$

2. It is given: $\|\boldsymbol{m}\| = 4;\ \|\boldsymbol{n}\| = \sqrt{2};\ (\widehat{\boldsymbol{m},\boldsymbol{n}}) = 135^0$. Find the norm of the vector $\boldsymbol{m} + 3\boldsymbol{n}$.

Solution.

For any vector $\boldsymbol{v}$, $\|\boldsymbol{v}\| = \sqrt{\boldsymbol{v}\cdot\boldsymbol{v}}$. Then we can find the norm of $\boldsymbol{m} + 3\boldsymbol{n}$:

$$\|\boldsymbol{m}+3\boldsymbol{n}\|=\sqrt{(\boldsymbol{m}+3\boldsymbol{n})\cdot(\boldsymbol{m}+3\boldsymbol{n})}=\sqrt{\boldsymbol{m}\cdot\boldsymbol{m}+3\boldsymbol{m}\cdot\boldsymbol{n}+3\boldsymbol{n}\cdot\boldsymbol{m}+9\boldsymbol{n}\cdot\boldsymbol{n}}=$$
$$=\sqrt{\|\boldsymbol{m}\|^2+6\|\boldsymbol{m}\|\cdot\|\boldsymbol{n}\|\cdot\cos 135^0+9\|\boldsymbol{n}\|^2}=\sqrt{16-24+18}=\sqrt{10}.$$

3. $\boldsymbol{a}$, $\boldsymbol{b}$, and $\boldsymbol{c}$ are three unit vectors satisfying the condition $\boldsymbol{a}+\boldsymbol{b}+\boldsymbol{c}=\boldsymbol{0}$. Evaluate $\boldsymbol{a}\cdot\boldsymbol{b}+\boldsymbol{b}\cdot\boldsymbol{c}+\boldsymbol{c}\cdot\boldsymbol{a}$.

Let us multiply the given condition $\boldsymbol{a}+\boldsymbol{b}+\boldsymbol{c}=\boldsymbol{0}$ by $\boldsymbol{a}$; we shall obtain $\boldsymbol{a}\cdot\boldsymbol{a}+\boldsymbol{a}\cdot\boldsymbol{b}+\boldsymbol{a}\cdot\boldsymbol{c}=0$. Similarly, by multiplying the given condition by $\boldsymbol{b}$ and $\boldsymbol{c}$ we can obtain: $\boldsymbol{b}\cdot\boldsymbol{a}+\boldsymbol{b}\cdot\boldsymbol{b}+\boldsymbol{b}\cdot\boldsymbol{c}=0;\quad \boldsymbol{c}\cdot\boldsymbol{a}+\boldsymbol{c}\cdot\boldsymbol{b}+\boldsymbol{c}\cdot\boldsymbol{c}=0$. Let us add the obtained three equalities: $\boldsymbol{a}\cdot\boldsymbol{a}+\boldsymbol{a}\cdot\boldsymbol{b}+\boldsymbol{a}\cdot\boldsymbol{c}+\boldsymbol{b}\cdot\boldsymbol{a}+\boldsymbol{b}\cdot\boldsymbol{b}+\boldsymbol{b}\cdot\boldsymbol{c}+\boldsymbol{c}\cdot\boldsymbol{a}+\boldsymbol{c}\cdot\boldsymbol{b}+\boldsymbol{c}\cdot\boldsymbol{c}=0$, which, taking into account that $\boldsymbol{a}\cdot\boldsymbol{a}=\|\boldsymbol{a}\|^2=1=\boldsymbol{b}\cdot\boldsymbol{b}=\boldsymbol{c}\cdot\boldsymbol{c}$ (since $\boldsymbol{a}$, $\boldsymbol{b}$, and $\boldsymbol{c}$ are unit vectors) and the commutative property of dot product, can be rewritten as

$$3+2(\boldsymbol{a}\cdot\boldsymbol{b}+\boldsymbol{b}\cdot\boldsymbol{c}+\boldsymbol{c}\cdot\boldsymbol{a})=0; \quad \Rightarrow \quad \boldsymbol{a}\cdot\boldsymbol{b}+\boldsymbol{b}\cdot\boldsymbol{c}+\boldsymbol{c}\cdot\boldsymbol{a}=-\tfrac{3}{2}.$$

It is interesting to observe the geometric meaning of this result.

First, let us notice that for a unit vector $\boldsymbol{u}$, its projection onto a vector $\boldsymbol{v}$ is equal to the cosine of the angle between $\boldsymbol{v}$ and $\boldsymbol{u}$: $\text{Proj}_{\boldsymbol{v}}\boldsymbol{u}=\|\boldsymbol{u}\|\cos\left(\widehat{\boldsymbol{v},\boldsymbol{u}}\right)=\cos\left(\widehat{\boldsymbol{v},\boldsymbol{u}}\right)$.

Also, a projection of a vector onto a unit vector is equal to their dot product (why?).

Vectors $\boldsymbol{a}$, $\boldsymbol{b}$, and $\boldsymbol{c}$ form a regular triangle with the sides of length 1(see the figure below). Then, $\boldsymbol{a}\cdot\boldsymbol{b}+\boldsymbol{b}\cdot\boldsymbol{c}+\boldsymbol{c}\cdot\boldsymbol{a}=\text{Proj}_{\boldsymbol{b}}\boldsymbol{a}+\text{Proj}_{\boldsymbol{c}}\boldsymbol{b}+\text{Proj}_{\boldsymbol{a}}\boldsymbol{c}=3\cos 120^0=-\tfrac{3}{2}$.

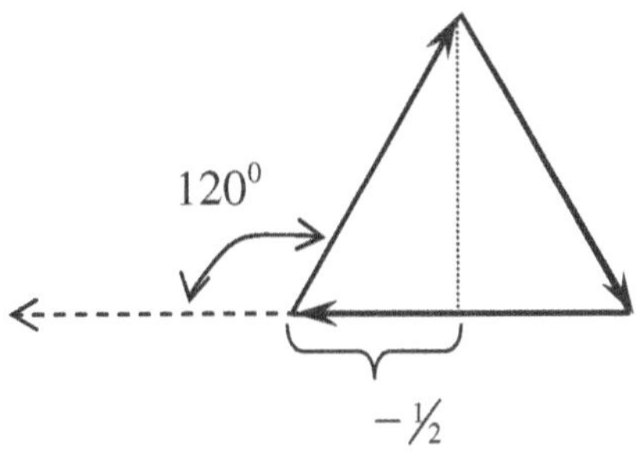

4. Vectors $\boldsymbol{a}$ and $\boldsymbol{b}$ are given by their coordinates in the standard basis $\{\boldsymbol{i},\boldsymbol{j},\boldsymbol{k}\}$:

   $\boldsymbol{a}$ = (1, -2, 2); $\boldsymbol{b}$ = (1, 0, 1). Find: (i) the orthogonal projection of $\boldsymbol{a}$ onto $\boldsymbol{a}-2\boldsymbol{b}$;

   (ii) an angle between $\boldsymbol{a}$ and $\boldsymbol{a}+\boldsymbol{b}$.

Solution.

$$\boldsymbol{a}-2\boldsymbol{b}=\begin{bmatrix}1\\-2\\2\end{bmatrix}-2\begin{bmatrix}1\\0\\1\end{bmatrix}=\begin{bmatrix}-1\\-2\\0\end{bmatrix}; \text{Then } proj_{\boldsymbol{a}-2\boldsymbol{b}}\boldsymbol{a}=\frac{\boldsymbol{a}\cdot(\boldsymbol{a}-2\boldsymbol{b})}{\|\boldsymbol{a}-2\boldsymbol{b}\|}=\frac{-1+4+0}{\sqrt{1+4+0}}=\frac{3}{\sqrt{5}}.$$

(It is not specified whether the scalar or vector projection to be found; the vector projection is $\overrightarrow{proj_{a\text{-}2b}a} = \frac{a\cdot(a-2b)}{\|a-2b\|^2}(a-2b) = \frac{3}{5}(a-2b) = \frac{3}{5}\begin{bmatrix}-1\\-2\\0\end{bmatrix}$).

We can determine the cosine of the angle: $\cos\left(\widehat{a,a+b}\right) = \frac{a\cdot(a+b)}{\|a\|\cdot\|a+b\|} = \frac{12}{3\cdot\sqrt{17}} = \frac{4}{\sqrt{17}}$.

5. Evaluate the area of a parallelogram formed by the vectors $3\boldsymbol{a}+\boldsymbol{b}$ and $\boldsymbol{a}-\boldsymbol{b}$, if $\|a\|=1;\ \|b\|=3;\ (\widehat{a,b})=30^0$.

Solution.

$$Area = \|(3a+b)\times(a-b)\| = \|(3a)\times(a)-(3a)\times(b)+b\times a-b\times b\| = \|-4a\times b\| =$$
$$= 4\|a\|\cdot\|b\|\sin 30^0 = 4\cdot 1\cdot 3\cdot\tfrac{1}{2} = 6\,[sq.units].$$

6. Vectors $\boldsymbol{a}$ and $\boldsymbol{b}$ are given by their components in the standard basis $\{i,j,k\}$: $\boldsymbol{a} = (2, -1, 1)$; $\boldsymbol{b} = (1, 0, -1)$. Find the unit vector perpendicular to both vectors $\boldsymbol{a}$ and $\boldsymbol{b}$ and forming an obtuse angle with the positive Y-semi-axis.

Solution.

A vector $\boldsymbol{v}$ perpendicular to $\boldsymbol{a}$ and $\boldsymbol{b}$ will be a scalar multiple of their cross product.

$v = a\times b = \begin{vmatrix} i & j & k\\ 2 & -1 & 1\\ 1 & 0 & -1\end{vmatrix} = i+3j+k$. Then a unit vector collinear with $\boldsymbol{v}$ will be

$$u_1 = \frac{1}{\|v\|}v, \text{ or } u_2 = -\frac{1}{\|v\|}v.\quad u_1 = \frac{1}{\sqrt{1^2+3^2+1^2}}\begin{bmatrix}1\\3\\1\end{bmatrix} = \begin{bmatrix}\frac{1}{\sqrt{11}}\\ \frac{3}{\sqrt{11}}\\ \frac{1}{\sqrt{11}}\end{bmatrix};\quad u_2 = \begin{bmatrix}-\frac{1}{\sqrt{11}}\\ -\frac{3}{\sqrt{11}}\\ -\frac{1}{\sqrt{11}}\end{bmatrix}.$$

Since the required vector forms an obtuse angle with the Y-axis, its second component must be negative (the cosine of an obtuse angle is negative); hence the required vector is $\boldsymbol{u}_2$.

7. Four points are given by their coordinates: $A(1, 0, 2)$; $B(0, 1, 3)$; $C(1, 1, -1)$; and $D(1, 1, 4)$.

   i. Evaluate the area of triangle BCD;

   ii. Determine, if these four points are lying in one plane;

   iii. Evaluate the volume of the pyramid $ABCD$.

Solution.

(i) The area is a half of the area of a parallelogram formed by any two vectors that represent sides of the triangle:

$$Area(\Delta BCD) = \left\|\overrightarrow{BC}\times\overrightarrow{BD}\right\| = \left\|\begin{vmatrix} \boldsymbol{i} & \boldsymbol{j} & \boldsymbol{k} \\ 1 & 0 & -4 \\ 1 & 0 & 1 \end{vmatrix}\right\| = \left\|-5\boldsymbol{j}\right\| = 5.$$

(ii) Four points are coplanar iff any four vectors joining all of them are coplanar. The latter are coplanar iff their triple product is zero.

$$\left(\overrightarrow{AB}, \overrightarrow{AC}, \overrightarrow{AD}\right) = \begin{vmatrix} -1 & 1 & 1 \\ 0 & 1 & -3 \\ 0 & 1 & 2 \end{vmatrix} = -5 \neq 0;$$ hence the points are not coplanar.

(iii) $Volume(ABCD) = \frac{1}{6}\left|\left(\overrightarrow{AB}, \overrightarrow{AC}, \overrightarrow{AD}\right)\right| = \frac{1}{6}\left|-5\right| = \frac{5}{6}.$

3. EQUATIONS OF LINES AND PLANES.

3.1 EQUATIONS OF LINES.

Parametric equations of Lines.

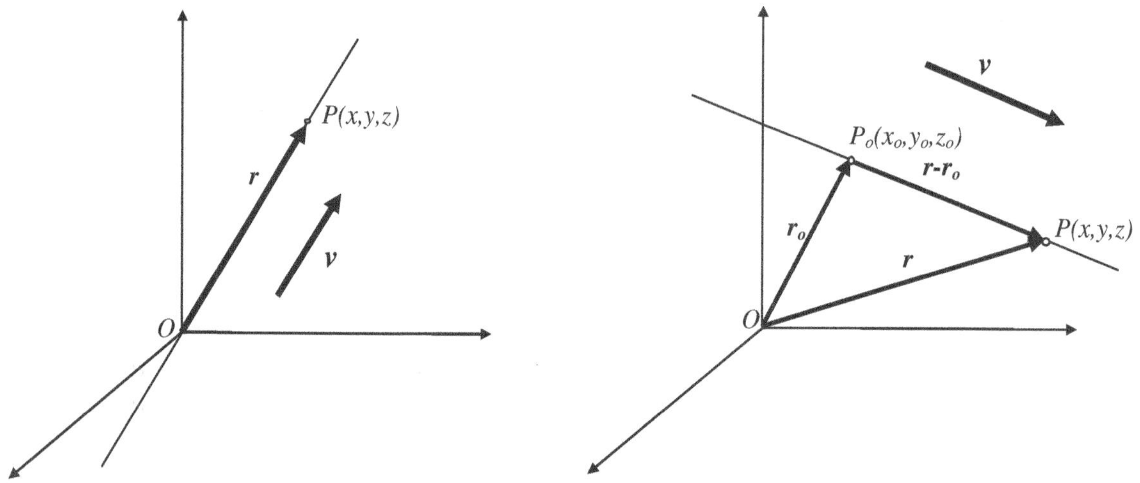

(a) (b)

Figure 1

A line is determined if we know a point lying in the line (it is called a *fixed point*) and the direction of the line. The latter is usually defined by a *direction vector*, a vector that lies in a line parallel to a given line, and thus is *collinear* to any vector lying in the given line. If two vectors are collinear, then each of them is a scalar multiple of the other (why?).

In Figure 1a a line that passes through the origin, *O*, is parallel to vector $\boldsymbol{v}$. Then, any vector joining *O* with a point in the line is a scalar multiple of $\boldsymbol{v}$, i.e.

$$\boldsymbol{r} = t\boldsymbol{v}, \tag{1}$$

where *t* is some number, usually called the *parameter.*

If $\boldsymbol{r} = (a, b, c)$ is a position vector of point P with coordinates *x, y, z* (such a point is called a *current point* of the line), one can rewrite equation (1) as a system of three scalar equations:

$$\begin{aligned} x &= at \\ y &= bt \\ z &= ct. \end{aligned} \tag{2}$$

Equations (1) and (2) are called, respectively, vector and scalar *parametric equations* of a line passing through the origin. Similarly, one can write the equations of a line that contains fixed point P_o (x_o, y_o, z_o) and is directed along vector $\mathbf{v} = (a, b, c)$ (see Figure 1b) as

$$\boldsymbol{r} - \boldsymbol{r}_o = \boldsymbol{v}t, \tag{3}$$

or

$$\begin{aligned} x - x_o &= at \\ y - y_o &= bt \\ z - z_o &= ct. \end{aligned} \qquad (4)$$

Physical interpretation.

One can deem equations (3), or (4) as equations of motion of a point moving from some point P_o with the velocity $\boldsymbol{v}$. Parameter t is interpreted as time. Then, by some moment t, the displacement of the point equals $\boldsymbol{v}t$.

One can exclude the parameter from the equations of a line. It follows from (4) that if none of the components of the direction vector is zero, t equals to each of the following ratios:

$$\frac{x - x_o}{a} = \frac{y - y_o}{b} = \frac{z - z_o}{c} \quad . \qquad (5)$$

The latter set of relations between the three coordinates of a point in a line is called the *symmetric* equations of the line. This is a system of three equations; each of them follows from the other two (only two of them are *linearly independent*).

3.2 EQUATIONS OF PLANES.

Parametric Equations of Planes.

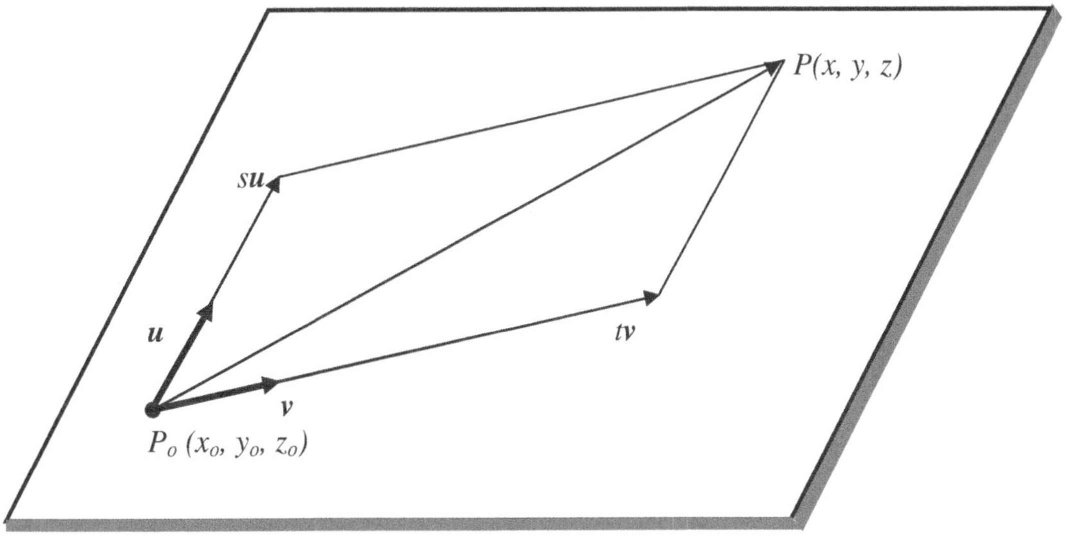

Figure 1

One can locate any point P in a plane, having given a fixed point P_o and two *non-collinear* vectors (that means: two vectors that are not lying on parallel lines) that lie in the plane or parallel to it. In Figure 1, P_o is a fixed point of a plane; its position vector is $\boldsymbol{r}_o$, and P is a current point of the same plane, and its position vector is $\boldsymbol{r}$. Then, vector $\overrightarrow{P_0P}$ can be expressed as

$$\boldsymbol{r} - \boldsymbol{r}_o = \boldsymbol{v}t + \boldsymbol{u}s\,. \qquad (6)$$

Example 1. A plane that contains point $P(1, 3, 4)$ and is parallel to the vectors $\boldsymbol{v} = (-1, 2, 1)$ and $\boldsymbol{u} = (3,0, 5)$ is described by the following parametric equations:

$$\begin{aligned} x-1 &= -t + 3s \\ y-3 &= 2t \\ z-4 &= t + 5s. \end{aligned} \tag{7}$$

Example 2. Write parametric equations of the line that is perpendicular to the plane from Example 1 and contains point $M(3, 1, 5)$.

Solution. A direction vector of the line is perpendicular to the vectors $\boldsymbol{v} = (-1, 2, 1)$ and $\boldsymbol{u}=(3, 0, 5)$, hence the cross product of these vectors, or any other vector that is collinear with their cross product, can serve as a direction vector.

$$\boldsymbol{u} \times \boldsymbol{v} = \begin{vmatrix} \boldsymbol{i} & \boldsymbol{j} & \boldsymbol{k} \\ -1 & 2 & 1 \\ 3 & 0 & 5 \end{vmatrix} = 10\boldsymbol{i} + 8\boldsymbol{j} - 6\boldsymbol{k}\ .$$

Then we choose $\frac{1}{2}(10, 8, -6) = (5, 4, -3)$ as a direction vector of the required line. Parametric equations of this line are:

$x - 3 = 5t;$

$y - 1 = 4t;$

$z - 5 = -3t.$ □

A Normal Equation of a Plane.

A plane may be defined by a point (called a *fixed point*) $P_o\ (x_o, y_o, z_o)$ lying in the plane, and a normal vector $\boldsymbol{N} = (A, B, C)$, which is perpendicular to the plane.

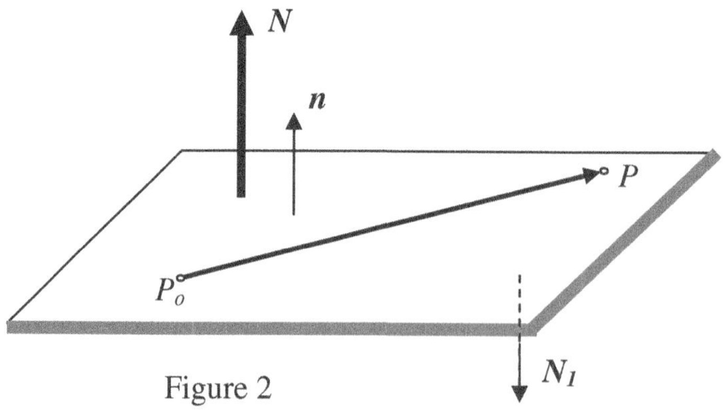

Figure 2

$\boldsymbol{N}$ is perpendicular to any vector joining the fixed point with any other (*current*) point of the plane, i.e. (see Figure 2)

$$\boldsymbol{N} \cdot \overrightarrow{P_0P} = 0. \tag{8}$$

Taking into account that

$$\overrightarrow{P_0P} = \boldsymbol{r} - \boldsymbol{r}_0, \tag{9}$$

the orthogonality condition (8) can be rewritten as

$$\boldsymbol{N}\cdot(\boldsymbol{r} - \boldsymbol{r}_0) = 0\,, \tag{10a}$$

or, in coordinate form,

$$A(x-xo) + B(y-yo) + C(z-zo) = 0. \tag{10b}$$

Either of equations (10) is called a *normal equation of a plane*. All normal equations of a plane are equivalent to each other, since all normal vectors (e.g., $\boldsymbol{N}, \boldsymbol{n}, \boldsymbol{N}_1$ in Figure 4) are collinear to each other and, thus, proportional to each other. After opening the brackets and rearranging the order of terms, (10b) can be written as

$$Ax + By + Cz + D = 0, \tag{11}$$

where

$$D = -(Ax_o + By_o + Cz_o). \tag{12}$$

A plane can be defined by (i) its parametric equations, or (ii) two lines lying in the plane, or (iii) three points contained in the plane. In each of these cases we know two vectors that are perpendicular to the normal vector of the plane, therefore it can be found as a cross product.

Example 3. Write a normal equation of a plane that contains the following points: M (1,0,2), N(-1,2,3), and P (4, 3, 5).

Solution. In order to solve the problem we have to know a normal vector of the plane. We can use the cross product of any two vectors that join the given three points to construct a normal vector, for example,

$$N = \overrightarrow{MN} \times \overrightarrow{MP} = \begin{vmatrix} \boldsymbol{i} & \boldsymbol{j} & \boldsymbol{k} \\ -2 & 2 & 1 \\ 3 & 3 & 3 \end{vmatrix} = 3\boldsymbol{i} + 9\boldsymbol{j} - 12\boldsymbol{k}\,.$$

Any of the given points, e.g. point M, can be chosen as a fixed point. Then, we obtain the following equation:

$$3(x-1) + 9(y-0) - 12(z-2) = 0.$$

We can reduce the equation by 3 (we could also choose ⅓$\boldsymbol{N}$ instead of $\boldsymbol{N}$ as a normal vector). The equation can be reduced to

$$x + 3y - 4z + 7 = 0.\ \square$$

Example 5. Find the distance from a given point $A(3, -1,5)$ to the plane given by its normal equation $2x - y + 2z - 2 = 0$.

Solution. We can view the distance from a point to a plane as the length of the projection of a vector joining the given point with any point of the plane onto a normal vector of the plane.

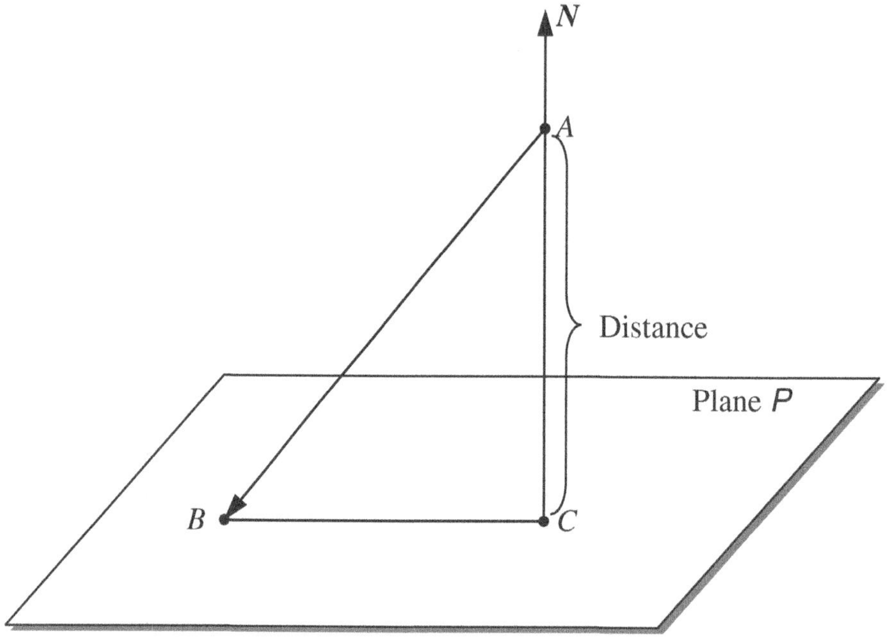

Figure 3

In Figure 3, point C is the foot of the perpendicular dropped from A onto the plane, hence AC is the required distance. Let B be an arbitrary point lying in the plane. Then, the required distance is equal to $AC = \left|proj_N \overrightarrow{AB}\right| = \left|\frac{\overrightarrow{AB} \cdot \boldsymbol{N}}{\|\boldsymbol{N}\|}\right|$.

B is an arbitrary point of the plane. Let for this point $x = y = 0$; then z can be found from the equation of the plane: $2 \cdot 0 - 0 + 2z - 2 = 0$, whence we can find $z = 1$. Thus, point B has the coordinates (0, 0, 1).

Then $\overrightarrow{AB} = \begin{bmatrix} 0 \\ 0 \\ 1 \end{bmatrix} - \begin{bmatrix} 3 \\ -1 \\ 5 \end{bmatrix} = \begin{bmatrix} -3 \\ 1 \\ -4 \end{bmatrix}$, and the required distance is

$$\left|\frac{\overrightarrow{AB} \cdot \boldsymbol{N}}{\|\boldsymbol{N}\|}\right| = \left|\frac{-3 \cdot 2 + (1)(-1) + 2 \cdot (-4)}{\sqrt{2^2 + (-1)^2 + 2^2}}\right| = \left|\frac{-15}{3}\right| = 5. \square$$

PRACTICE PROBLEMS (Section 3: Equations of Lines and Planes)

1) Write parametric and symmetric equations of the line through (2,1,1) that is perpendicular to the plane $x - 3y + z + 7 = 0$. Find the point of intersection of the line with the *YZ*- plane.

2) Write parametric equations of the plane that is parallel to the lines L: $x = t - 1$, $y = 2t - 2$, $z = 3t$ and l: $x = s - 1$, $y = 6$, $z = s + 2$ and contains the point $P(1, -1, 4)$.

3) Write the parametric equations of the plane passing through the origin O (0,0,0) parallel to the plane containing points (1, 0, 3), (2, 1, 0), and (1, 1, 1).

4) Write a normal equation of the plane described in the problem #3. Use this equation to write another set (different from the one you've obtained in #3) of parametric equations for this plane.

5) Write a normal equation of the plane passing through point M (2, 1, 6) parallel to the y-axis and to the line L connecting the origin with the point P (2, 0, 5).

6) Find the distance from the point $P(1, 0, 5)$ to the plane given by the equation $x - 2y + 2z - 5 = 0$.

SOLUTIONS TO PRACTICE PROBLEMS (Section 3)

1. Any vector perpendicular to the plane, e.g. the normal vector (1, - 3, 1) from the given equation, may serve as a direction vector of the line. The equations of the line are:

$$\begin{bmatrix} x \\ y \\ z \end{bmatrix} = \begin{bmatrix} 2 \\ 1 \\ 1 \end{bmatrix} + t\begin{bmatrix} 1 \\ -3 \\ 1 \end{bmatrix}; \qquad \frac{x-2}{1} = \frac{y-1}{-3} = \frac{z-1}{1}.$$

In order to find the point of intersection with the plane $x=0$, we can use either set of the equations. For example, let us use parametric equations. $x=0; \Rightarrow 2+t=0; \Rightarrow t=-2.$ Then we substitute this value of t in the parametric equations for y and z: $y=1+(-2)(-3)=7;\ z=1+(-2)1=-1.$
The point of intersection is (0, 7, -1).

2. Since the plane is parallel to the lines, their direction vectors are direction vectors of the plane. Then, the parametric equations of the plane through (1, -1, 4) with direction vectors (1, 2, 3) and (1, 0, 1) are:

$$\begin{bmatrix} x \\ y \\ z \end{bmatrix} = \begin{bmatrix} 1 \\ -1 \\ 4 \end{bmatrix} + p\begin{bmatrix} 1 \\ 2 \\ 3 \end{bmatrix} + q\begin{bmatrix} 1 \\ 0 \\ 1 \end{bmatrix},$$ where p and q are the parameters.

3. Any two out of six vectors connecting the given three points can be chosen as direction vectors of the plane. For example, we can choose
(2, 1, 0) – (1, 0, 3) = (1, 1, -3) and (1, 1, 1) – (1, 0, 3) = (0, 1, -2).
The equations we obtain are:

$$\begin{bmatrix} x \\ y \\ z \end{bmatrix} = \begin{bmatrix} 0 \\ 0 \\ 0 \end{bmatrix} + t\begin{bmatrix} 1 \\ 1 \\ -3 \end{bmatrix} + s\begin{bmatrix} 0 \\ 1 \\ -2 \end{bmatrix}, \quad \text{or} \quad \begin{bmatrix} x \\ y \\ z \end{bmatrix} = t\begin{bmatrix} 1 \\ 1 \\ -3 \end{bmatrix} + s\begin{bmatrix} 0 \\ 1 \\ -2 \end{bmatrix}.$$

4. We can use the cross product of direction vectors of the plane as a normal vector of the plane:

$$\boldsymbol{N} = \begin{vmatrix} \boldsymbol{i} & \boldsymbol{j} & \boldsymbol{k} \\ 1 & 1 & -3 \\ 0 & 1 & -2 \end{vmatrix} = \boldsymbol{i} + 2\boldsymbol{j} + \boldsymbol{k}.$$

Then the normal equation of a plane passing through the origin with this normal vector will be
$x + 2y + z = 0$.
This equation can be solved with respect to, e.g. x; then y and z are free parameters of the solution. The general solution of this equation can be written as
$x = -2p - q;\ \ y = p;\ \ z = q,$
which is another set of parametric equations of the plane.

5. Since the plane is parallel to the y-axis and vector $\overrightarrow{OP}$, the vectors $\boldsymbol{j} = (0, 1, 0)$ and $\overrightarrow{OP} = (2, 0, 5)$ are direction vectors of the plane. Then, their cross product will be a normal vector of the plane:

$$N = \begin{vmatrix} \boldsymbol{i} & \boldsymbol{j} & \boldsymbol{k} \\ 0 & 1 & 0 \\ 2 & 0 & 5 \end{vmatrix} = 5\boldsymbol{i} - 2\boldsymbol{k}.$$

The corresponding normal equation will be $5(x-2) - 2(z-6) = 0$, or $5x - 2z + 2 = 0$.

6. Let us find a point lying in the plane. Then the distance from P to the plane is the magnitude of the orthogonal projection of the vector joining the found point with P onto a normal vector of the plane.

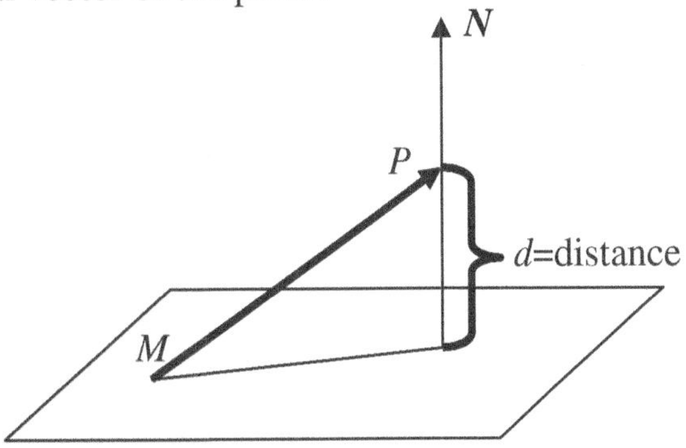

Let us choose for the coordinates of point M lying in the plane: $y = z = 0$; then, from the equation of the plane, we find $x = 5$. So, the coordinates of M are (5, 0, 0). Then $\overrightarrow{MP} = (1-5, 0-0, 5-0) = (-4, 0, 5)$.

$$d = \left|\frac{\overrightarrow{MP} \cdot N}{\|N\|}\right| = \left|\frac{(-4, 0, 5) \cdot (1, -2, 2)}{\sqrt{1+4+4}}\right| = \frac{6}{3} = 2.$$